Einzelgän

Stoicism for Inner Strength

Edited by Fleur Marie Vaz

Copyright © 2023 by Einzelgänger

All rights reserved. This book or any portion thereof may not be reproduced or used in any manner whatsoever without the express written permission of the publisher except for the use of brief quotations in a book review.

ISBN: 9798854189552
Printed by Amazon Kindle Direct Publishing

First print, August 2023

www.einzelganger.co

Thank you supporters and subscribers.

– Einzelgänger

Contents

Introduction 5

Part I: Foundations of Stoicism   10

    Chapter 1   Physics, Ethics & Logic 11

    Chapter 2   Virtues, Vices & Indifferents 23

    Chapter 3   The Passions 38

Part II: Building Blocks to Inner Strength (the Stoic Way)   51

    Chapter 4   Mental Toughness 53

    Chapter 5   Fortitude 60

    Chapter 6   Success 71

    Chapter 7   Calm in Uncertainty 80

    Chapter 8   Suffering in Imagination 89

    Chapter 9   Not Clinging 103

    Chapter 10   Being a Loser 113

    Chapter 11   Unconquerable 124

    Chapter 12   Degenerates 132

    Chapter 13   Feeling Harmed 141

    Chapter 14   Aging 152

    Chapter 15   Self-Discipline 160

    Chapter 16   Future, Past, Present 170

    Chapter 17   Embrace Fate and Live Well 180

Introduction

In ancient times, the Roman author and linguist Aulus Gellius found himself aboard a ship, accompanied by a Stoic philosopher. Dark clouds gathered above the sea, warning of an impending storm. The waves grew increasingly wild, hurling saltwater onto the deck as the ship's crew labored diligently to maintain their course. Suddenly, a flash of lightning illuminated the sky, immediately followed by the most deafening clap of thunder Aulus had ever heard. Some passengers screamed in terror, while others cried openly. Aulus turned to the Stoic philosopher at his side, expecting to find him unperturbed. To his astonishment, although the philosopher neither cried nor shouted, his body quivered, his complexion was as pale as the moon, and his anxious eyes were fixed upon the threatening waves in the distance.

Once the storm had subsided, Aulus confronted the Stoic philosopher, asking him why he couldn't stop his emotional response to the storm from happening. After all, the Stoics train themselves to be tranquil in the face of the external world. The philosopher, however, explained that certain bodily reactions can arise spontaneously and unexpectedly when confronted with sudden potential danger, even before one's intellect and reason have a chance to intervene. Hence, even the wisest may grow pale for a while when surprised by a swift clap of thunder, as they haven't begun to process it. Nevertheless, shortly after the storm's initially terrifying displays, the Stoic philosopher recognized that everything occurs in accordance with nature and that there is no cause for fear. Consequently, his equanimity was swiftly restored.

Even after a couple of millennia, misconceptions persist about the goals of practicing Stoics. Many people imagine a Stoic as an emotionless being with the demeanor of a rock. While it's true that Stoics aim to avoid experiencing the passions—fully-formed emotions based on flawed reasoning—they don't seek to eradicate emotion altogether. A well-trained Stoic may lack the emotional entanglement that many 'ordinary' or 'untrained' individuals possess. For example, remorse is an emotion that a true Stoic sage would banish from their repertoire, as it is always based on a mistaken mindset, according to their philosophy. But it's not a Stoic's goal to be entirely devoid of emotions.

These are reasonable non-problematic emotional reactions, such as the proto-emotional responses that Aulus Gellius observed in the philosopher during the storm. Moreover, the ancient Stoics recognized three positive emotions called *eupatheia*, which arise when one lives 'in agreement with nature.' So, being without passions doesn't mean being completely without emotions. The philosopher's inner strength didn't lie in his initial bodily reaction, but in the way he used reason to swiftly restore his composure in the face of a major storm.

As I refined my essays for publication, I noticed that reducing the passions lies at the root of most of them, just like in my previous compilation, *Stoicism for Inner Peace.* I don't think that's a surprise. Even though a Stoic's ultimate goal is 'living in agreement with nature,' a major aspect of what the Stoics tried to accomplish is a state of, what we could call, 'unperturbedness.' Being overwhelmed by the passions always finds root in a certain desire or aversion to external things. Hence, when we encounter what we desire, we're elated but when we don't, we're disappointed. And when we incur what we're averse to, we feel miserable, but when we avoid it, we're relieved.

Do you see the issue here? The problem is that because of these attachments and aversions, we let external circumstances dictate how we feel. Often, the heaviness of the passions decides our actions as well. We may cower in fear when we should act, or lash out in anger when compassion and understanding are more constructive. We may spend the years after a traumatic event in tremendous, debilitating grief, wasting the potential for a good life.

This capacity to remain (largely) unswayed by the external world while maintaining inner tranquility is what I would describe as inner strength. Possessing inner strength allows us not only to withstand life's numerous adversities but also to achieve our goals by remaining committed. The chapters of this book contemplate Stoic philosophy and their wisdom as a source and guiding light toward inner strength; to reduce the passions though reason without becoming lifeless rocks. While I have extensively drawn upon classic Stoic texts and modern literature on the ancient philosophy founded by Zeno of Citium, much of my content is interpretative—essentially a product of extrapolating from original Stoic ideas to create formats that address everyday situations and contemporary issues. Questions such as how to remain calm amid uncertainty, how to become unconquerable, and why attempting to control our surroundings is futile are explored within these discussions.

The following chapters contain collected essays that originally served as scripts for my YouTube videos. Initially, I did not intend them to be cohesive, as I considered them momentary reflections that emerged from specific times and places, informed by the knowledge I possessed at those moments. However, when compiling this book I came to realize that they are nonetheless part of a single, contemplative journey. Hence, my editor Fleur Marie Vaz and I have done our best to turn these essays into a unified, step-by-step guide that reveals the fundamentals of Stoic inner strength.

To add more depth and clarity to my writings, I've created three introductory chapters that briefly explain the foundations of Stoicism. I'll admit that these explanations far from entail the complete and ever evolving corpus of Stoic philosophy, but, hopefully, they're instrumental in grasping the Stoic way of thinking. My hope is that reading this book will provide you with answers to life's uncertainties, drawn from the rich and profound wisdom of the ancient Stoics.

Einzelgänger

Part I: Foundations of Stoicism

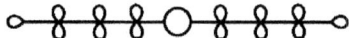

Stoicism as a philosophical school is comprehensive and vast, containing detailed descriptions on the workings of the universe, a system of logic and detailed explanations on how to behave ethically. Physics, logic and ethics form the three pillars of Stoic philosophy. Even though logic and physics are essential parts, the ethics are often considered the fruits of the philosophy—the good stuff.

I've noticed during my YouTube presence that most of my audience is particularly interested in Stoic ethics. Questions they seem to seek answers to are: How can this philosophy bring me inner peace? How can Stoicism help me through adversity? How can Stoic wisdom help me become successful in my work? These questions I've been asking as well (especially the first one) and they all fall into the ethics category. Hence, the emphasis of the second part of the book lies on ethics.

Yet, before you delve into the subsequent chapters, I believe it's important to have at least some basic knowledge about the system as a whole. This especially covers the Stoic theories of emotions, virtues and vices (which are central themes of the ancient Stoic texts). That's why I recommend you to read these basics of Stoicism first.

Chapter 1   Physics, Ethics & Logic

As a philosophical system, we can divide Stoicism into three pillars *(topos): physics, ethics,* and *logic.* Some scholars arrange these aspects of Stoicism in the form of an egg. The yolk represents the physics, the white the ethics, and the shell the logic. The metaphor of the egg clarifies the idea that physics, ethics and logic are interdependent parts of a whole, emphasizing that the one cannot function without the other. The same is true for the metaphor of the garden, coined by the Greek philosopher Chrysippus (considered the greatest of Stoics, whose work, unfortunately, only survives in fragments). The fence represents logic which, like the eggshell, protects the inside of the garden. The soil or yolk represents physics that possesses the power of fertility, namely, the knowledge and understanding of the world. This, in turn, gives birth to the white or fruits called ethics.

Let's stick with the egg. Without the core, the yolk (physics), it's difficult to determine the ethics, as these are based on the nature of reality. How can we decide what behaviors lead to a good life, without knowledge of the workings of the universe? Hence, the workings of the cosmos should be clear as they form a Stoic's guiding light. We cannot determine the best way for a human being to live, if we don't know how human beings work. We cannot decide how to best handle our emotions, if we lack the knowledge of how they operate. And so it's impossible to create a functional ethical system for life if we have no idea of how life actually works.

I must clarify, though, that Stoic views on how the world works have been changed and updated throughout the centuries, implying that nothing is set in stone. Their theories of 'matter' and *pneuma* may sound outdated and scientifically unfounded, as they may not align with current scientific knowledge. Lacking the scientific tools and knowledge we have today, the ancient Stoics tried to make sense of the world as many still try to do two millennia later. I'd say that the essence of physics is an understanding of the workings of the universe, encapsulating everything from our solar system, to the elements, to human behavior.

And then there's logic. Without it, we cannot understand ethics and physics. Logic allows us to comprehend patterns, cause and effect, and the difference between probable and improbable. The use of logic is prevalent in Stoic scriptures, like in the *Enchiridion* which is a manual containing the fundamental teachings of Epictetus, who is considered one of the most influential Stoic philosophers. When reading the *Enchiridion* (which was compiled by Epictetus' student Arrian) we see how logic is part of the fabric of Epictetus' utterances. Through logic, he makes a distinction between things that are up to us and things that aren't up to us, and the consequences of this observation, exposing the reality of how limited human power is in the face of the cosmos. Also, using logic, Epictetus shows us the futility of desire and aversion regarding things that aren't up to us, stating:

> *If the only things you try to avoid are things that really are under your own control, then you'll never have to take what you wanted to avoid. But if you try to avoid illness or poverty or death, you're bound to be miserable, sooner or later.*

Epictetus, *Enchiridion*, 2 (translated by Stephen Walton)

So, by knowing the 'what' (physics) we can determine the 'how' (ethics). But we can only determine the 'how' using logic. To further clarify physics, ethics and logic, we'll briefly explore each of these pillars individually.

Physics

Again, in short, Stoic physics is the understanding of the universe. Even though Stoic physics differs significantly from the physics we find in the great religions such as Christianity and Islam, there are similarities. For example, both Christians and Muslims acknowledge a divine order in the universe. Whereas they propose God as creator and sustainer, the ancient Stoics described a concept called the *Logos*, that is, a rationally operating principle that governs the universe. Of course, the big difference here is that Christianity and Islam are monotheistic (the belief in one God), while Stoicism is a pantheistic philosophy (all is God). Also, the Christian and Islamic God is personal, omnipotent and omniscient, while the Logos represents an impersonal, all-pervasive force that shapes the universe. It is not a personal deity who actively intervenes in human affairs—let alone communicates privately with us. Yet, quite inconsistently, this impersonal force is frequently personified in the ancient Stoic texts as 'Zeus' or 'Fortuna,' or simply 'the gods,' in reference to ancient Greek deities.

Nonetheless, like God, Logos has a plan. What this plan is, we don't know. The universe indeed acts in mysterious ways, from a human perspective, but from a Stoic viewpoint everything that happens—no matter how unfortunate—is ultimately part of the divine scheme. What's our role in it? We, as humans, are to live in agreement with it, which is considered ethical and therefore the goal of any Stoic.

According to the Stoics, existence is based on matter and *pneuma*, which we could consider the material manifestations of Logos. Matter is everything our senses can perceive, but is passive and lifeless in itself, and also destructible. On the other hand, *pneuma,* the active force behind the ever-changing manifestation of the cosmos, is completely mingled with the passive matter and cannot be destroyed. Chrysippus described pneuma as the "vehicle" of Logos that structures matter. Simply put, pneuma makes the universe alive. In her book, *Stoicism and Emotion*, author Margaret Graver describes pneuma as "a highly energized gaseous material." Even though, according to the Stoics, pneuma consists only of fire and air, it has extraordinary capacities. The movement of stars and planets, the existence of life, the waves of the sea, all are propelled by pneuma and based on the rational principle of Logos.

What about human choice? The ancient Stoics believed that the path of existence has been pre-determined. However, they also argued that there are countless different realities, depending on what choices we make, and hence there are many different paths to follow. Thus, we still have a choice. This choice is referred to as 'will' or 'moral purpose' or 'moral choice' *(prohairesis)* and is the only thing we humans have complete control over and can even override the power of the gods. Epictetus makes this clear during one of his lectures, saying:

> *My leg you will fetter, but my moral purpose not even Zeus himself has power to overcome.*
>
> Epictetus, *Discourses*, 1.1 (translated by W.A. Oldfather)

Ethics

Since we have a choice, this leads us to a discussion of ethics. The early Stoa described the ethical life as "living in agreement with nature." To many, this sounds extremely vague. It also sounds an awful lot like a concept from Taoism, as in, "going with the flow" or "following Tao." But the Stoics have created a comprehensive system that explains what living in agreement with nature means, and how we can put it into practice.

Living in agreement with nature is synonymous with living virtuously. A person that masters perfect virtue, the Stoics refer to as a "sage" or "wise man," even though such an individual is very rare. Some argue that even Epictetus, one of the most respected Stoics from the later era, wasn't a fully actualized sage himself, although he must have been advanced on that path. So, practicing Stoics aren't required to be sages; it's the commitment to the path that makes a *prokoptôn, that is,* a Stoic disciple making progress.

This book focuses on the ethics-side of Stoicism. Despite the importance of logic and physics, the ethics is the useful and practical part and considered the fruits of the philosophy.

The goal of following the Stoic ethical system is to arrive at a state of flourishing, which the Stoics called *eudaimonia*. Eudaimonia is an optimal state of being which includes inner peace and tranquility, even during great adversity, because there's no intellectual resistance to Fate. I believe that this freedom from emotional pain as a consequence of hardship is what attracts most people to Stoicism. It's what motivated me at least, to study this ancient philosophy and apply its wisdom to my life. An individual experiencing eudaimonia doesn't wish for things to happen as he wants, but as they happen. As a consequence, whatever happens is according to what he wishes and, therefore, he'll never be harmed by unexpected circumstances or experience emotional pain.

However, there's more to Stoicism than being emotionally resilient. The Stoics seek to be engaged with the world and act in ways that benefit the whole. Doesn't that sound a bit paradoxical? On the one end, they seek emotional independence from external circumstances and, on the other, they are fully participating in it. I think this is where the virtuous side of the Stoics truly comes to fruition: to act well, consistently, without being attached to the outcome. And so, in any situation, the focus lies on the act itself, rather than what we can get out of it. After all, the results are beyond our control.

But how do we act well, according to Stoicism?

The Stoic system of virtue and vice offers guidance. It provides us with four cardinal virtues and four corresponding cardinal vices which are also divided into sub-categories. The value of these virtues and destructiveness of these vices are often addressed, directly or subtly, in the ancient texts. For example, Epictetus spoke of the importance of honesty and integrity in his lectures. And the Stoic emperor Marcus Aurelius regularly argued that human beings are made to be industrious. The next two chapters will go deeper into these virtues, vices and the gray area that lies in between.

Logic

The Greek philosopher Chrysippus largely developed the Stoic system of logic. Apparently he wrote more than 300 books about the subject, which are all lost except some fragments. Therefore, unfortunately, there isn't much knowledge about it. But the ancient texts show us that the Stoics used logical reasoning to explore and explain the physical world and to determine the best ways to operate in it. When it comes to the Stoic egg, we could say that logic is not just the hard shell that holds ethics and physics together, but also the firm and solid art of reasoning that creates our understanding of physics and ethics. Thus, without logic, the ethics and the physics departments would fall apart, like an egg without a shell.

Stoic logic includes language rules, like propositions that are either good or false.

Take for example, the proposition:

It is light.

If it is indeed daytime, this proposition is true. But in the middle of the night, this proposition is false. To explain this, we can add a bit more complexity to the argument and make the following proposition:

If it is day, it is light.

But it gets even more exciting. Out of these propositions we can make arguments. In Stoic logic we find so-called 'syllogisms' that do exactly that. A syllogism is a type of logical argument that uses deductive reasoning to reach a conclusion based on two propositions (or premises, to be precise) that are claimed or assumed to be true. As an example (*modus ponens*):

If it is day, it is light.
It is day.
Therefore, it is light.

We'll not go too deeply into the system of propositions and syllogisms as I think it's too heavy for this paragraph. My goal here is to briefly show the Stoic use of logic in their reasoning, exploration of the world, and creation of ethics. When reading ancient Stoic texts, we'll encounter this logic repeatedly in their arguments. Take, for example, the logic of cause and effect presented by Epictetus' quote earlier:

> *If the only things you try to avoid are things that really are under your own control, then you'll never have to take what you wanted to avoid. But if you try to avoid illness or poverty or death, you're bound to be miserable, sooner or later.*

Epictetus, *Enchiridion*, 2 (translated by Stephen Walton)

Epictetus based his propositions on a core Stoic concept: the *dichotomy of control*. The dichotomy of control reveals that some things are up to us and others are not. Such observation lies in the realm of physics: it's the knowledge of how things work, in this case, the degree of control we have, as humans, over "things." So, now we know this, what's the correct course of action if we seek inner peace? Here's what we should keep in mind according to Epictetus:

> *Remember that desire demands the attainment of that of which you are desirous; and aversion demands the avoidance of that to which you are averse; that he who fails of the object of his desires is disappointed; and he who incurs the object of his aversion is wretched.*

Epictetus, *Enchiridion*, 2 (translated by T.W. Higginson)

In this passage, Epictetus refers to things outside of our control. He explains that desire and aversion regarding these things have consequences, namely, if we fail to attain what we're desirous of or encounter what we're averse to, we'll suffer. The reason we run the risk of not attaining what we want, or of encountering what we avoid, is that these things are not in our control. Therefore, Epictetus called them weak, slavish, restrained and belonging to others. They're unreliable and, therefore, the Stoics consider them inferior sources of happiness. So, the logic solution would be to only desire and be averse to things we can control.

> *If, then, you shun only those undesirable things which you can control, you will never incur anything which you shun; but if you shun sickness, or death, or poverty, you will run the risk of wretchedness.*

Epictetus, *Enchiridion*, 2 (translated by T.W. Higginson)

The logic behind Epictetus' statements (based on physics) immediately translates to a piece of advice that we can place in the realm of ethics: *"Remove aversion, then, from all things that are not in our control, and transfer it to things contrary to the nature of what is in our control."*

What then are the things that are considered virtues and vices in the Stoics' universe? This leads to our next discussion.

Chapter 2   Virtues, Vices & Indifferents

A Stoic's ultimate aspiration is to attain the *eudaimonia* we just discussed. Eudaimonia is that flourishing state that emerges when we live in harmony with nature. But what does it mean to live in harmony with nature? Zeno of Citium stated that living "in agreement" (to which Cleanthes, Zeno's successor later added "with nature") is living in accordance with reason. From a metaphysical viewpoint, we can view nature as an overarching cosmic force, an all-encompassing plan based on a perfect rational principle. This perfect rational plan is Logos; this the ancient texts often refer to as the will of Zeus, or Fate. The *Stanford Encyclopedia of Philosophy* explains that, according to the Stoics, living in agreement with all-compassing, cosmic nature, requires attuning one's own reason with that of the whole cosmos.

The "perfected condition" of human reason is *virtue*. In essence, virtue is the pathway to a happy, flourishing life, in other words, eudaimonia. But what does it mean to be virtuous? Are there any rules or guidelines? Luckily, yes. The Stoics provided a detailed description, making sense out of the rather vague idea of 'living in agreement with nature' and 'virtue.'

Virtue

A Stoic aspires to live virtuously. For them, virtue is the *only* thing that ever contributes to happiness. This vastly contradicts today's societal perception of what makes people happy, which often depends on external objects and events like wealth or a happy marriage. From a Stoic point of view, such external objects and events are 'indifferents,' meaning that they, in themselves, don't contribute to happiness (we'll explore these 'indifferents' in the next chapter). In addition, these things are not in our control, while virtue, and thus, happiness, is.

Of course, the next question that comes to mind is: What is virtue? Stoicism uses a system that proposes four cardinal virtues. These cardinal virtues were adopted from Plato, but the Stoics gave their unique interpretation to them. They are: *wisdom*, *temperance*, *justice* and *courage*. Each virtue has sub virtues, but in academia there seems to be a lack of consensus as to which are the correct sub virtues, since there are different sources (like Diogenes Laërtius and Arius Didymus) that list different virtues. However, there seems to be consensus regarding the validity of the four cardinal virtues as being the pillars. The same goes for the four opposing vices, which we'll explore in a bit.

According to the Stoics, to be happy and flourishing individuals, we must possess all four virtues, which are interconnected and form a unity. This means that if one possesses *one* virtue, one possesses *them all*, and that a virtuous person automatically gravitates toward all four virtues. The Stoics used an example to illustrate this idea: just as a single individual can be an orator, poet and general while still remaining one person, so can different virtues be a applied in different areas of life but still be unified.

Vice

The corruption of reason, or vice, is the sole thing that causes unhappiness and it is "bad" or "evil." Succumbing to these elements will lead us astray. Just like the Stoics considered virtue the sole contributor to happiness, so is vice the only thing that leads to unhappiness. Again, such a stance goes against contemporary views regarding what human unhappiness entails, as we can quickly point to unfortunate external circumstances like loss, poverty or illness as prime sources of unhappiness. The 'cardinal vices' are: *foolishness*, *intemperance*, *injustice* and *cowardice*. Vice in itself is a form of ignorance; a misguided approach to life that is adopted irrespective of external circumstances.

As you probably have noticed, the vices are the opposites of the cardinal virtues. Let's look at some of these dichotomies.

(1) Wisdom and foolishness

The (peer-reviewed) *Internet Encyclopedia of Philosophy (IEP)* subdivides wisdom into good calculation, discretion, quick-wittedness, resourcefulness and good sense. John Stobaeus, who compiled a series of extracts from Greek authors, described wisdom as "knowledge of what one is to do and not to do and what is neither."

As a cornerstone of the Stoic virtues, wisdom allows us to understand both our choices and the consequences of them. We can ask: What is not only beneficial for ourselves, but also for the people around us? What makes us happy and what doesn't? Are our thoughts rational or based on the passions? A wise person has an understanding of how the world works (but also recognizes the limitations of this understanding) and has knowledge about how to navigate this world. It is no wonder that Stoic literature abounds with wisdom on a myriad subjects.

So how do we acquire wisdom? Through both experience and study. Through his lectures while teaching in school in Nicopolis, Epictetus continually shared his wisdom. Arrian, one of his students, took a vast amount of notes during these lectures, which later became the *Enchiridion* and *Discourses*. Quite interestingly, Epictetus emphasized the importance of study during one of his talks, mentioning three fields of study that someone who wishes to excel and be "good" (in the Stoic sense) must be trained in:

The first has to do with desires and aversions, that he may never fail to get what he desires, nor fall into what he avoids; the second with cases of choice and of refusal, and, in general, with duty, that he may act in an orderly fashion, upon good reasons, and not carelessly; the third with the avoidance of error and rashness in judgement, and, in general, about cases of assent.

Epictetus, *Discourses*, 3.2 (translated by W.A. Oldfather)

In contrast to a wise person, a fool engages with the world in ways that are detrimental to both themselves and their environment. Foolishness entails making improper decisions and taking actions that are not grounded in sound judgment and accurate knowledge. A fool doesn't recognize "what one is to do and not to do and what is neither." For example, chasing short-term pleasures such as drinking and partying in the pursuit of happiness can grow into a destructive addiction. And, by clinging to an impermanent universe, our mood depends on Fortuna's whims, placing us in an unreliable position. (By way of background, Fortuna refers to the ancient deity, Fortuna, the goddess of chance, luck, and fate, which the ancient Stoics often referred to when they spoke about fate.)

Also, by being extremely selfish, and acting at the cost of other people, we'll eventually harm ourselves as well. For we are an inseparable part of the whole, just like limbs on a body.

(2) Justice and injustice

Justice in the Stoic view goes beyond what is typically seen as legal or social justice. It embraces a broader understanding similar to jurisprudence, which focused more on how people should treat each other ethically. The IEP subdivides justice into honesty, piety, fair dealing and equity. This shows us that the Stoics didn't aim at creating a judicial system of some sort. Rather, they were concerned about the harmony and well-being of humanity as a whole. Stobacus described justice as "knowledge of the distribution of proper value to each person."

Justice entails treating others with kindness, compassion and respect, and recognizing their inherent dignity and rights. It involves fulfilling our social obligations and contributing to the well-being of the community and society as a whole. The just person seeks to create a harmonious and cooperative social order, promoting the common good and upholding moral principles. According to the Stoics, we cannot be happy and flourishing beings if we undermine the whole by treating others badly.

Injustice, on the other hand, harms not only the world around us but ourselves. When we are unfair, disloyal, and untrustworthy, people distance themselves from us. Moreover, engaging in acts of injustice such as cheating and slander can erode our moral compass, causing us to lose sight of what is right and wrong.

Marcus Aurelius wrote:

> *Injustice is a kind of blasphemy. Nature designed rational beings for each other's sake: to help—not harm—one another, as they deserve. To transgress its will, then, is to blaspheme against the oldest of the gods.*

Marcus Aurelius, *Meditations*, 9.1 (translated by Gregory Hays)

In his *Discourses*, Epictetus puts a man who committed infidelity in his place. He confronts him with the consequences of his "unjust" actions (corresponding with violating the sub-virtues of 'honesty' and 'fair dealing,' we could say). This results in a loss of trust by his environment, and being considered "useless." Epictetus, quite harshly, compares him to a wasp: people tend to run away from these creatures, and even try to swat them because of their tendency to sting. Of course, the way people treat you is typically something you can't control, and, therefore, isn't the main problem here. The problem lies in the detrimental effects of one's unjust actions on others, i.e., the whole.

Why do people behave unjustly? It often comes down to excessive desires. Consider the issue of greed, for example. Greed is an excessive preoccupation with one's self-preservation, driven by the belief that one requires far more than one actually needs. A greedy person is never satisfied and will often enrich themselves at the expense of others, employing dishonesty and a lack of integrity. In today's world, we witness the consequences of greed and the accompanying injustice, which undermine the quality of life for many people, animals, and the environment as a whole. All this occurs because an insatiable minority constantly seek more. This tendency corresponds with the vice 'intemperance.'

(3) Courage and cowardice

Courage is the virtue that enables us to face challenges, adversity, and fear with bravery and resilience. It is not limited to physical courage but encompasses moral courage as well—the ability to act in accordance with our values and principles, even in the face of opposition or hardship. The courageous person is willing to take risks, confront difficult situations, and stand up for what is right, regardless of the potential consequences. Courage enables us to overcome our fears and insecurities, to persevere in the pursuit of virtue, and to act in alignment with our highest ideals.

The IEP subdivides courage into endurance, confidence, high-mindedness, cheerfulness, and industriousness. I agree, that characteristics like 'cheerfulness,' 'endurance,' and 'industriousness' don't quite resemble today's meaning of the word 'courage.' It shows that the Stoic meaning of courage is broader, and could, perhaps, better be described today as 'fortitude.' It's fortitude that allows us to continue in difficult tasks, and maintain moral courage in situations that challenge our moral values. We could also say that fortitude aids us in being (realistically) optimistic and confident in the face of adversity, and not letting life's hardships tear us down.

Cowardice, on the other hand, doesn't contribute to our own well-being or that of the whole. Virtuous actions require courage. If we fail to speak out against oppression and injustice, refuse to take action or to work diligently to build a better world, if we shy away from acting virtuously, our collective progress as a species will be hindered. Cowardice, in many cases, will negatively impact our individual lives as well. It is often said that people tend to regret the things they haven't done more than the things they have. When we lack courage (or fortitude), we risk stagnation, unfulfillment, and a life filled with regret. Or worse, we could lose ourselves at the hands of addictions, as we lack the fortitude and faith in ourselves to confront them.

In a letter to his friend Lucilius, Stoic philosopher and statesman Lucius Annaeus Seneca, also known as Seneca the Younger, wrote:

> *It is not because things are difficult that we do not dare; it is because we do not dare that they are difficult.*

Lucius Annaeus Seneca, *Moral Letters to Lucilius*, 104 (translated by Richard M. Gummere)

(4) Moderation and intemperance

Moderation, also known as temperance or self-control, is the virtue that governs our desires, emotions, and actions. The IEP subdivides moderation into seemliness (taking other's needs into consideration), modesty, discipline and self-control. Moderation involves finding a balanced and harmonious approach to life, and avoiding extremes and excesses in our thoughts and behaviors. The moderate person exercises self-restraint and discipline, avoiding over-attachment to material possessions and excessive indulgence in pleasure. By cultivating moderation, we can avoid being enslaved by our desires and impulses, which hinders virtue.

In contrast, intemperance is a vice closely related to the pursuit of so-called 'indifferents' (explained in the next chapter). Intemperance is the excessive indulgence in pleasures and the accumulation of desires, material goods or power or status, often at the expense of moderation and self-control. The ancient Greek philosopher Epicurus argued that the right amount of pleasure leads to happiness, emphasizing the importance of moderation. For instance, a modest amount of wine can bring enjoyment, while excessive consumption results in a hangover and consequent discomfort. The misuse of indifferents—such as overindulgence in food, excessive television or binge-watching streaming platforms—leads to unhappiness in the long run.

Intemperance is also a manifestation of greed, which is often intertwined with injustice and foolishness. Consequently, an intemperate lifestyle is detrimental to the collective good, as it frequently exploits others. Many workers experience poverty and deplorable working conditions, receiving meager wages to satisfy someone else's over-indulgence.

For the individual, we can observe that a life of intemperance does not bring happiness. Continually seeking to gratify our desires through food, drink, or promiscuous sexual behavior implies that we search for fulfillment in external sources, while true contentment can only be found within. Thus, we exhaust ourselves and our environment in a futile quest for satisfaction. By practicing self-control and moderation, we not only benefit ourselves but also contribute positively to the world around us.

To sum up this chapter, let me quote from Seneca's essay *On the Shortness of Life*:

> *Vices beset us and surround us on every side, and they do not permit us to rise anew and lift up our eyes for the discernment of truth, but they keep us down when once they have overwhelmed us and we are chained to lust.*

Lucius Annaeus Seneca, *On the Shortness of Life*, chapter II (translated by John W. Basore)

So what do we do when we are thus so weighed down by vices that we cannot look up to perceive the truth? For a part, the answer is in categorizing some things as 'indifferents' and changing the way we view them.

Indifferents

We saw earlier that in the Stoic ethical system, not everything in life can be put into the virtue or vice boxes. There's a massive gray area containing elements that the Stoics consider neither beneficial nor harmful in themselves, which can be classified as 'preferred' or 'dispreferred' indifferents. Examples of preferred indifferents are: strength, wealth, health, a good reputation, and social connections. Examples of dispreferred indifferents are: disease, weakness, ugliness (as in, unattractive bodily features), poverty, and low reputation.

Although indifferents can significantly impact one's life, they neither negate the opportunity to live virtuously nor the risk of falling into vice. Wealthy individuals may lead exceptionally destructive lives, while those in poverty can exemplify virtuous living. Even the severest of adversities like imprisonment and torture can still allow virtue. As virtue doesn't depend on these indifferents, the Stoics consider them neither good nor bad.

The nature of indifferents is that they are ultimately not up to us. They belong to what Epictetus' dichotomy of control categorizes as 'not within our control.' Therefore, making them the focal point of our lives isn't a great idea if we seek to be free from suffering.

> *The things in our control are by nature free, unrestrained, unhindered; but those not in our control are weak, slavish, restrained, belonging to others. Remember, then, that if you suppose that things which are slavish by nature are also free, and that what belongs to others is your own, then you will be hindered.*

Epictetus, *Enchiridion*, 1 (translated by Elizabeth Carter)

Still, the indifferents have a role to play. The Stoics recognize that humans naturally incline towards preferred indifferents, as they can support and even enhance the pursuit of virtue. Naturally, we want our bellies full and, if possible, we'd like to own preferred indifferents such as large houses, and have a substantial amount of savings in our bank account. The word 'preferred' signifies that people naturally gravitate towards them, and so, as is stated in the IEP, "selecting them is *usually* commended by reason." After all, wouldn't Zeus have meant for people to select what's in their best interests, thus, health over illness and wealth over poverty? Hence, we could say that selecting preferred over dispreferred indifferents is 'in agreement with nature,' even though lady Fortuna doesn't always give us what we want.

Although not directly reflected in the four cardinal virtues we've explored in the previous chapter, a characteristic of the virtuous agent is *apatheia*, a state commonly translated as 'equanimity.' Equanimity is a consequence of being virtuous, which Epictetus repeatedly described as "freedom," specifically from the passions. We generally create unfreedom through how we approach indifferents. If we're unreasonably attached to preferred indifferents, for example, to our stock market investments or to significant others, we let our 'happiness' depend on the whims of Fate. This isn't true happiness according to the Stoics, as it implies a slavish dependency on preferred indifferents.

When we think of it, we realize that the 'illusory' happiness we experience when we have access to the things we desire involves the fear of losing that access just as, conversely, the happiness of not having encountered the things we're averse to involves the fear of encountering them perhaps somewhere in the future.

So far we have talked about virtues and vices and neutral conditions such as indifferents. All these affect our feelings and emotions to a large extent but what have the Stoics to say about our emotions? Is being stoic being a rock without emotion?

Chapter 3   The Passions

I think there's a widespread misunderstanding about what it means to be stoic, and what Stoics aim to achieve in regards to their emotional state. This could be the case because in certain languages the world 'stoic' signifies someone who doesn't complain or show their emotions. However, there's a difference between a Stoic (with a capital letter 'S') and being stoic. The first one points to a practitioner of Stoicism. The second one points to an attitude or, more of an external presentation of oneself, a pose of being indifferent and non-emotional but also joyless to some extent in certain circumstances.

So, when thinking of a 'Stoic,' many people imagine a marble statue that just stands there cold in the face of adversity—non-reactive, non-responsive and emotionless. This view of a 'Stoic' isn't entirely accurate.

The point is Stoicism isn't about eradicating all emotions. When it comes to emotions, it's about curbing what they call the 'passions' (*pathê*). These passions are subdivided in four main categories: *distress (lupē), fear (phobos), lust (epithumia),* and *delight (hēdonē).* We'll explore these categories and subcategories later in this chapter.

But first, what's the difference between emotions and passions? It's slightly complicated. In her book, *Stoicism and Emotion*, Margaret Graver sticks with the term 'emotion' when talking about the Stoic passions, as the word better fits the actual substance of what the ancient Stoics called *pathê*. For example, the Stoics categorize grief and anger as 'passions,' but most English speakers will probably agree that we'd call them 'emotions.' Although I think Graver makes a strong argument for her choice, I'd prefer to keep using passions for the sake of consistency as I've used the term in other essays as well.

According to the Stoics, the passions are a consequence of our judgment of our circumstances, be it events that happened in the past, our current state of affairs or things that might happen in the future. These judgments occur in the ruling-faculty (*hêgemonikon*). Epictetus' explained this mechanism effectively, by saying:

> *Men are disturbed not by things, but by the views which they take of things. Thus death is nothing terrible, else it would have appeared so to Socrates. But the terror consists in our notion of death, that it is terrible.*

Epictetus, *Enchiridion*, 5 (translated by T.W. Higginson)

A wrong judgment about our circumstances generates a passion. The most basic way to explain what a 'wrong' judgment entails is to say that it's any judgment that contradicts the course of the universe. The 'universe' in this context is the totality of things that aren't within our control, as mentioned at the beginning in Epictetus' *Enchiridion*: "body, property, reputation, command, and, in one word, whatever are not our own actions." Death, for instance, is a completely natural event and, therefore, not bad or terrible. If our judgment contradicts the (correct) notion that there's nothing wrong with death, then a passion arises. The same goes for people splashing water and being rude in the bathhouse, as it's the 'nature' of bathing.

So, it's not the circumstances in themselves that cause the passions, but the way we judge these circumstances. Logically, we curb the passions by correcting our judgments. Sounds familiar? In that case, you might have heard of *Cognitive Behavioral Therapy (CBT)*, which focuses on replacing irrational with rational thoughts.

The Passions explained

So do the Stoics consider the passions a consequence of irrational thinking. Behind every passion hides a thought process that doesn't conform to the Stoic ideal that the external world is nothing of our concern. Then what is of our concern? Things within our control, like pursuit, opinions, desire, aversion, restraint—whatever our own choices are able to control. So it's not the world that decides our mood, but our attitude towards it. If we let the world determine our mental state, we experience the passions: we concern ourselves with things outside our control; and so, we become their servants instead of our own master.

What are the Stoic passions and what are their possible destructive consequences? The Stoics distinguish *four* passions: distress, fear, lust, and delight.

Distress (*lupē*)

Distress is an irrational reaction to what's happening in the present, coming from the opinion that what's happening is terrible and shouldn't be happening. The cause of distress is our belief that the present moment is, somehow, loathsome. But is it? According to the Stoics, whatever happens outside of us is neutral. It's our thoughts about such outside circumstances that make them loathsome. That's why people have different reactions to the same situation: for one person, it evokes distress, while it hardly moves another. An example of this is the philosopher Epicurus who died painfully because of a stone in the bladder, but remained cheerful.

Fear (*phobos*)

The second one is fear. Fear is another irrational aversion or avoidance regarding things that we believe could or will happen in the future. Like distress, the passion of fear arises when we believe that the thing we might encounter is, somehow, terrible. But it's our thoughts that make it terrible, not the thing itself. Where fear differs from distress is that, when we're fearful, we oppose something that lies in the future. We experience 'anticipatory anxiety,' as the thing we fear hasn't even arrived yet. By so doing, we avoid many situations which could lead to missed opportunities and failing in our duties.

Seneca wrote beautifully in a letter to his friend:

There are more things, Lucilius, likely to frighten us than there are to crush us; we suffer more often in imagination than in reality.

Lucius Annaeus Seneca, *Moral Letters to Lucilius*, 13.4 (translated by Richard M. Gummere)

Lust (*epithumia*)

The third passion is lust. The ancient Stoics saw lust as the irrational desire for things we want and could obtain in the future. Lust signifies a preoccupation with something not in our control. When we're lustful, we burden ourselves with a strong desire that seeks fulfillment. And when we fail to encounter what we lust after, we're disappointed. The world pulls the lustful person in all directions like a donkey following a carrot on a stick, sometimes with terrible consequences. Seneca stated:

> *But among the worst cases I count also those who give their time to nothing but drink and lust; for these are the most shameful preoccupations of all.*

Seneca, *On the Shortness of Life*, chapter VII (translated by John W. Basore)

Delight (*hēdonē*)

The fourth one is delight or pleasure. Delight is the irrational enjoyment of something in the present, coming from the opinion that what's happening is good and enjoyable. Like the way distress corresponds with fear, delight corresponds with lust. If we delight in something, we will likely lust after it when the thing or situation we delight in is absent. This absence can lead to cravings and addiction, which are antithetical to equanimity. Also, after we delight in something, we always need more to achieve the same level of pleasure, so we risk falling into a bottomless pit.

In the table below you'll see how the passions relate to either 'good' or 'bad' prospects in the present and the future. The 'good' and 'bad' in the context of this table refers to the experiential value and not the moral value of the passions.

	Present	**Future**
Good	Delight	Lust
Bad	Distress	Fear

Non-problematic emotions

But curbing the passions doesn't mean being without emotion. There are other types of emotion that the Stoics don't count as passions.

Firstly, there are emotions as a consequence of mental illness which the one who experiences them cannot influence with reason. Secondly, there are so-called 'proto-emotions' which the Stoics considered emotions that aren't fully formed, and involuntarily arise in the body in certain situations. For example, an explosion will usually startle you initially, before you can put your ruling-faculty to work. We earlier saw how the Roman author Aulus Gellius mentioned a philosopher on a sailing ship, who panicked and paled when a storm occurred. When people asked him to explain his reaction, he grabbed the fifth volume of Epictetus' *Discourses* out of his bag and said:

> *When some terrifying sound occurs, either from the sky or from the collapse of a building or as the sudden herald of some danger, even the wise person's mind necessarily responds and is contracted and grows pale for a little while, not because he opines that something evil is at hand, but by certain rapid and unplanned movements antecedent to the office of intellect and reason. Shortly, however, the wise person in that situation 'withholds assent' from those terrifying mental impressions; he spurns and rejects them and does not think that there is anything in them which he should fear.*

Aulus Gellius, *Noctes Atticae (Attic Nights)*, 19.1.14

The fifth volume of Epictetus' *Discourses* is lost, unfortunately. But from this passage, Epictetus' distinction between *passions* and *proto-emotions* becomes clear. Proto-emotions appear instantly and randomly as a reaction to a first impression. Thus, they aren't the problem. However, how we deal with them could be problematic. In his book *Of Anger*, Seneca explains the subtle difference between proto-emotions and passions as well:

> *None of these things which casually influence the mind deserve to be called passions: the mind, if I may so express it, rather suffers passions to act upon itself than forms them. A passion, therefore, consists not in being affected by the sights which are presented to us, but in giving way to our feelings and following up these chance promptings.*

Lucius Annaeus Seneca, *Of Anger*, 2.3 (translated by Aubrey Stewart)

Aside from the proto-emotions, the Stoics recognized 'good-feelings' (*eupatheia*) as non-problematic emotions. We could see these 'good-feelings' as alternatives for the passions. For lust, there's *wish*, for delight, *joy*, and for fear, *caution*. For distress, however, there is no replacement. These emotions are reasonable *and* of moderate quality, as they generally don't overwhelm a person. For example, we can *wish* ourselves a healthy life. But we also can be accepting when illness strikes us, instead of *lusting* after "health" and being devastated with a different outcome. Or even better: instead of wishing a healthy life, we could *wish* to have the strength to deal with illness when it occurs. Below you can see how the good-feelings relate either 'good' or 'bad' prospects in the present and future.

	Present	**Future**
Good	Joy	Wish
Bad	-	Caution

Evoking the passions

Imagine a husband cheating on his wife (who happens to be a Stoic sage), and the wife catches him in the act. Her initial reaction could be full fright, perhaps even tears; these are the previously explored proto-emotions at work. But her well-trained mind quickly puts the situation in its right perspective. Judging from a place of reason, it reminds her that there's no reasonable ground to be upset.

But what if she doesn't judge from a place of reason? In that case, she might think: "This shouldn't have happened to me! I don't deserve this! This is so unjust!" Even though we could sympathize with such emotions, they are fundamentally at odds with the nature of existence, which shows that these things do happen. Existence includes all kinds of adversities like death, illness and betrayal, and no one comes into this world with some divine lawful exemption from these things. Even Jesus Christ, Son of God, suffered immensely. When we look at reality we see that cheating and betrayal happen all the time. And often, it happens to the best of us.

From a Stoic viewpoint, we could therefore ask: Why would we be upset at something natural and all too common? Is such a triviality worth affecting our equanimity, especially in the long term?

But, clearly, most people don't think this way. Our default position seems to be one of well-defined desires and aversions and corresponding reactions. We believe that our sadness and anger are appropriate when we encounter something we're averse to, and that delight and craving are the proper reactions to something we desire. Moreover, many believe that some things should happen and others shouldn't, implying entitlement. "I shouldn't be sick," we might think. Or, "I deserve only the best." Of course, no one is entitled to a 'desired outcome,' over just an 'outcome.' Yet, we do get emotional when we don't get what we think we deserve, and encounter what we think we don't deserve.

Now, the deeper we fall into the endless void of desire and aversion, chasing and avoiding, clinging and repelling, the more we evoke the passions.

Curbing the passions

How then can we prevent the passions from overwhelming us? The works of the ancient Stoics are a goldmine of wisdom on how to reach and maintain an equanimous state.

One of the central themes within Stoicism is the acceptance of Fate. Hence, Epictetus tells us not to demand that things happen *as we wish* but *as they happen.*

By doing so, we'll be content with what comes our way; we won't desire anything other than what Fate provides us, nor will we be averse to anything. With such an attitude, passions have no ground to stand on.

What reason is there to desire or fear anything if we're already guaranteed to get what we want? What reason is there for distress when we don't wish circumstances to be different regardless of these circumstances? And what's the reason for delight in something particular, if everything else is okay too (even though not preferred)? Thus, simply put, we neutralize our passions by neither wanting so much from the world nor avoiding or opposing anything. Epictetus had a simple solution that fortifies us against desire and aversion: treat the world with moderation and restraint.

> *It's like a banquet, with dishes going around. If something tasty stops in front of you, take some if you want. If it hasn't reached you yet, don't grab for it. If it misses you entirely, don't make a fuss. Take the same attitude toward family, money and position. Partake of them as they come to you and there's no blame.*

Epictetus, *Enchiridion,* 15 (translated by Stephen Watson)

But, of course, to abstain from grabbing for all these goodies isn't easy, especially in a world that constantly bombards us with opportunities for delight. The key is practice, meaning that we have to train our attitudes to strengthen them. For every desire and aversion that we wish to conquer, there's an inner quality that we can develop, so we'll eventually get a firmer grip on our passions. For temptations that arouse lust and desire, we have self-control. For adversity, we have optimism, or 'seeing the silver lining;' we also have endurance. For fear and avoidance, there's courage. For unfriendly, ignorant, and disrespectful people, there's compassion and patience.

Part II: Building Blocks to Inner Strength (the Stoic Way)

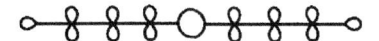

How do we build resilience the Stoic way? What did the ancient Stoics say about fortitude? How do we achieve success? How can we cope with the prospect of aging and death and the uncertainties of the future? How do we deal with a world of winners and losers?

The following chapters explore a variety of reflections on Stoic philosophy concerning the common theme of inner strength. Fortitude is a Stoic virtue, which is reflected in the ancient texts. But I've come to see that Stoic inner strength is multifaceted. Living virtuously, or in agreement with nature, plays an essential role here. Among virtue, the Stoics counted industriousness, moderation toward pleasures, and also honesty. From a Stoic perspective, the sum of virtue makes a resilient, well-rounded, happy person.

For myself, the logical and rational approach of the Stoics helped me most in dealing with adversity in life: the realization of what's not in my power, the transience of pleasures and hardships, the meaninglessness of worrying so much about other people's opinions, and the inescapability of illness and death. It's the repetitive reflection of these truths and mindfulness of my thoughts and "impressions" that has provided me with strength.

Hopefully, the contemplations you'll find in the coming chapters will be a source of resilience and strength.

Chapter 4   Mental Toughness

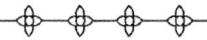

The ancient Stoics aimed to be resilient towards the things beyond their control and were set on their path of virtue (see chapter 2: Virtues, Vices & Indifferents). Mental toughness is necessary to be truly 'good' in the Stoic sense, as we need to be strong enough to control destructive desires, to choose virtuous activities over vices and to *anchor* ourselves in the present moment. In everyday life, mental toughness also allows us to reach our goals and effectively navigate through dire straits. How did the Stoics achieve this level of mental resilience?

(1) The power within surpasses even the gods

Seneca and Socrates died in a similar fashion. Both were sentenced to death and, in both cases, the execution or 'forced suicide' was to take poison. But the most striking shared characteristic was the calmness by which they left the world. Death is just another phenomenon that isn't up to us since nature creates and takes life at will. The same goes for losing the people we're attached to, things we might be offended by, and injustice that may befall us. In the end, it's nature (or God) that decides the workings of the external world. Not us.

For many people, this realization could evoke a sense of powerlessness. In part, this seems reasonable. The good news, however, is that we have complete control over the greatest strength of all, which is our choice (or *prohairesis* which we use as part of and in conjunction with the ruling-faculty).

As Epictetus described in the Enchiridion: "Things in our control are opinion, pursuit, desire, aversion, and, in a word, whatever are our own actions." This power is the essence of mental toughness, which is a muscle that can be trained. Possessing complete power over our own actions, as far as that power applies in a certain moment, makes our will untouchable, even by the gods.

People can inflict damage on us, or humiliate us. But even so, we can maintain that power over our attitudes and the actions that follow. In his *Discourses*, Epictetus emphasized that people can impact his life only to a certain degree—they're only limited to the realm outside of himself. To quote the Stoic philosopher:

> *I must die: must I, then, die groaning too? I must be fettered: and wailing too? I must go into exile: does anyone, then, keep me from going with a smile and cheerful and serene? "Tell your secrets." I say not a word; for this is under my control. "But I will fetter you." What is that you say, man? fetter me? My leg*

you will fetter, but my moral purpose not even Zeus himself has power to overcome.

Epictetus, Discourses, 1.1 (translated by W.A. Oldfather)

(2) Overcoming the unnatural tendencies of laziness and procrastination

As human beings, we've never been so comfortable as we are now with all the benefits of technology at our disposal. But too much comfort can lead to stagnation and even the deterioration of the human spirit, as observed by Marcus Aurelius, once emperor of the world's most powerful empire. Now, the following discourse may not be for everyone since it's heavily based on Stoic beliefs about nature.

The Stoics aim for living in accordance with nature. Of course, our human nature has set limits (that vary from person to person) to how much sleep we need, how much food we need, how much movement we need, and so on, in order to function properly. Most people that spend days on the couch watching Netflix with a bucket of ice cream do this probably because it feels nice and comfy. But, according to Marcus Aurelius, this is not the natural way of living for a human being and, therefore, it's wrong. To quote the Stoic emperor:

So you were born to feel "nice"? Instead of doing things and experiencing them? Don't you see the plants, the birds, the ants and spiders and bees going about their individual tasks, putting the world in order, as best they can? And you're not willing to do your job as a human being? Why aren't you running to do what your nature demands?

Marcus Aurelius, *Meditations*, 5.1

So, according to the Stoics, you don't love yourself enough if you're lazy, because if you did, you'd love your nature too. And it's your nature, they believe—this flame within, that shouts at you to make something out of your life and live in a virtuous manner. An antidote for laziness is the cultivation of courage. Courage is a Stoic type of virtue that can be subdivided into endurance, confidence, high-mindedness, cheerfulness, and industriousness. These states are part of the eudaimonic 'flourishing' experience or the Stoic concept of happiness. So, considering that laziness and procrastination are unnatural and that we're born to play a part in the whole, or to be concerned with "putting the world in order" as Marcus states, courage can be a huge mental boost.

Simply put: we feel our best when we flourish and we do not feel our best when we're lazy and stagnant.

(3) Contentment is strength

We find ourselves in a very unstable position if our happiness depends on external circumstances. That's why Stoic sages don't excessively desire or cling to external things for happiness, as these sources are unreliable and not their own. Foolish people, on the other hand, are in a constant state of wanting, while being oblivious of what they truly need. They are in a position of weakness, easily manipulated by their surroundings. According to the Stoics, we don't need *"all those things for which men pray"* to be content and happy. So, what do we need? Not much, as far as the Stoics are concerned. As Seneca put it:

> *I shall tell you what I mean by health: if the mind is content with its own self; if it has confidence in itself; if it understands that all those things for which men pray, all the benefits which are bestowed and sought for, are of no importance in relation to a life of happiness; under such conditions it is sound. For anything that can be added to is imperfect; anything that can suffer loss is not lasting; but let the man whose happiness*

> *is to be lasting, rejoice in what is truly his own. Now all that which the crowd gapes after, ebbs and flows. Fortune gives us nothing which we can really own.*

Lucius Annaeus Seneca, *Moral Letters to Lucilius*, 72.7

Tremendous strength lies in this state of wholeness and self-sufficiency. From the vantage point of our contemporary world, this strength manifests as resilience against social expectations and the pressures of consumerism. If we're strong enough to steer clear from the many temptations that the world has to offer, we'll be less swayed by them, and more able to focus on things that truly matter to us. Advertisements of products we don't need, smooth talk by used car salesmen, and useless commercial trends will barely sway us. But what's a Stoic to enjoy then? How about the joy of not wanting anything else but the present in all its imperfections?

As I'm getting older, I increasingly experience how contentment ultimately happens in my mind—not with the external circumstances I seek to acquire. When I look back on my younger years, I realize how my mind had tricked me into believing that happiness always implies some goodie to be acquired—some external conditions to be realized. For example, in my twenties I couldn't stand spending my weekends alone and was out partying at least twice a week (often more). Partying at least once a week was required to be content in my mind. But as we speak, me pushing forty, spending time alone in my apartment with food in the fridge, my couch, my desk, and access to the internet and my bookcase sometimes makes me feel the happiest man alive. Partying wasn't a requirement after all. It was simply another thing *"which the crowd gapes after"* that I believed was necessary to feel content.

However, I do have my weak spots. I can be relentlessly ambitious when it comes to my creative pursuits, to the point of suffering, even though I know very well that ultimately that's not where happiness lies. From a Stoic perspective, there's still plenty of room for improvement in that area of my life. But I've experienced that being content with few material goods makes me mentally tough, in the sense that I'm not easily conquered by the many temptations of our consumerist society.

Chapter 5   Fortitude

There's a world of difference between facing a situation with fortitude and retreating into a fortress. When we choose the latter, we often isolate ourselves physically, attempting to escape the harsh realities of the world. It's not unlikely that serial self-isolators suffer from feelings of powerlessness, believing that what's happening outside is too much for them, as they lack the strength and skill to cope. Unfortunately, they miss out on many life experiences, simply because they do not want to face the malevolence of humankind.

Now, there's another way to go about this. Instead of self-isolation, we could choose to strengthen our faculties, meaning that we become more resilient towards unpleasant people and situations, and don't let them stop us from living a good life. How can Stoic principles help us transform our mindset and develop fortitude? Let's explore what different Stoics of antiquity had to say about this virtue.

(1) Seneca

Firstly, it is important to recognize that our beliefs and expectations can sometimes create significant distress in our lives. It's not life itself that causes us pain, but rather our beliefs about how life should or shouldn't be.

The logic behind this is that we often tie our happiness to certain expectations and when these expectations repeatedly do not come to fruition because they don't align with an undeniable and inevitable reality, we suffer.

An example of this can be found in a letter that Stoic philosopher Seneca wrote to his friend Serenus. Serenus wished that people wouldn't treat each other with rudeness and scorn. But Seneca explained to him that this is the wrong way to look at it:

> *You are expressing a wish that the whole human race were inoffensive, which may hardly be; moreover, those who would gain by such wrongs not being done are those who would do them, not he who could not suffer from them even if they were done.*

Lucius Annaeus Seneca, *On The Firmness Of The Wise Man*, IV

Thus, by changing how we look at the world, we relieve ourselves of the pain of resistance. Life is full of pain, and full of people that are rude, selfish, and violent. The less we resist this fact, the more we can face the world in a tranquil manner. In his work *Of Peace of Mind*, Seneca argued that we cannot live well if we don't know how to die well. If we know that death is the fate that was laid upon us the moment we were born, we will live according to it. This realization adds to our mental fortitude: knowing that we could die anytime; nothing can befall us unexpectedly. He wrote:

> *For by looking forward to everything which can happen as though it would happen to him, he takes the sting out of all evils, which can make no difference to those who expect it and are prepared to meet it: evil only comes hard upon those who have lived without giving it a thought and whose attention has been exclusively directed to happiness. Disease, captivity, disaster, conflagration, are none of them unexpected: I always knew with what disorderly company Nature had associated me.*

Seneca, *Of Peace of Mind*, XI

(2) Epictetus

Epictetus teaches us the foundation of mental fortitude, which is the curbing of our desires and aversions. Most people that interact with the world desire certain outcomes. This isn't necessarily a bad thing, but such a stance has its consequences. Epictetus stated:

> *He who is making progress, having learned from philosophers that desire means the*

> *desire of good things, and aversion means aversion from bad things; having learned too that happiness and tranquility are not attainable by man otherwise than by not failing to obtain what he desires, and not falling into that which he would avoid; such a man takes from himself desire altogether and defers it, but he employs his aversion only on things which are dependent on his will.*

Epictetus, *Discourses*, 1.4 (translated by W.A. Oldfather)

The above idea very much applies to everything we do. As Epictetus states in the *Enchiridion*, things beyond our control are weak and slavish. And if we let our mood depend on things that are not up to us, we find ourselves in quite a vulnerable position. Therefore, according to Epictetus we should be indifferent towards anything independent of our own will. Because if we aren't, we will let external factors rule over our ability to be happy.

Mental fortitude, therefore, entails a healthy contempt for the things beyond our control; things we normally approach with desire or aversion. This means ceasing to desire that people should like you, ceasing to be averse to losing your possessions, and focusing entirely on your own actions. Epictetus goes as far as to say that we should even wish to be ridiculed, despised, if that preserves our peace of mind. He stated:

> *You must watch, you must labor, you must get the better of certain appetites, must quit your acquaintance, be despised by your servant, be laughed at by those you meet; come off worse than others in everything, in magistracies, in honors, in courts of judicature. When you have considered all these things round, approach, if you please, if, by parting with them, you have a mind to purchase equanimity, freedom, and tranquility.*

Epictetus, *Enchiridion*, 29 (translated by Elizabeth Carter)

(3) Chrysippus

Chrysippus made great contributions to Stoic philosophy; particularly in regards to the Stoic system of propositional logic. He was quite an industrious man, having written more than 700 volumes. Unfortunately, none of them survived. Chrysippus further expanded on the Stoic system of ethics, and followed the idea that living a happy life is the end goal which all of our actions should be geared towards. And to reach this goal, we should examine the universe to find out what's good and bad. Or how he put it:

> *... to live in accordance with one's experience of the things which come about by nature.*

Chrysippus, SVF1.12

From this point of view, the Stoics gave birth to a system that differentiates between virtue, vice and everything that's in between. They concluded that living virtuously means living happily, and living in vice means living unhappily (see chapter 2: Virtues, Vices & Indifferents). One of the cardinal Stoic virtues is 'courage' (as opposed to 'cowardice,' which the Stoics consider a vice). Courage can be considered an essential element of building Stoic fortitude.

Oftentimes, the path of virtue requires us to confront our fears, and go through pain instead of avoiding them. Courage allows us to make the right choices, and reach our goals despite the obstacles on our path. Typical everyday vices are 'quick fixes.' Using substances immoderately, or replacing challenging tasks by easily digestible pleasures, are ways in which we cower from difficult situations. The problem is that, though vices bring short term pleasure, that is immediately followed by the misery of not reaching our long-term goals. And so we gamble away opportunities we're too afraid to take. The inevitable low that follows an action that isn't good for us and our environment often manifests in shame and guilt.

Virtue, on the other hand, may involve temporary discomfort, but, from the Stoic perspective, the long-term satisfaction we gain is worth the struggle. Therefore, we could see virtue as a star in the sky that we continuously aim for. Moreover, by anchoring ourselves in a goal that transcends pain and pleasure, it's much easier not to falter in the face of adversity. This mindset requires an indifference towards the external situation we're in, not letting it overshadow our faculty of choice. Thus we focus primarily on our own actions, and whether or not they're virtuous. What's happening around us is secondary, as it's a matter of fate, which is beyond our control.

> *But if I really knew that it was ordained for me to be ill at this present moment, I would even seek illness: for the foot also, if it had a mind, would seek to be covered with mud.*

Chrysippus, as quoted by Epictetus, *Discourses*, 2.6 (translated by W.A. Oldfather)

In fact, sickness to the body, or whatever else may overcome us, doesn't impede our ability to act. According to the Stoics, what happens is how nature has intended it to be. So we shouldn't wish for things to happen differently; instead we should accept it and do what's best in that given situation. This accepting position towards fate, and how this benefits fortitude, leads us to the next Stoic philosopher and former Roman emperor, Marcus Aurelius.

(4) Marcus Aurelius

As the leader of the world's largest empire, Marcus Aurelius knew exactly how harsh life could be. Rome was not only in continuous war with its enemies, it was also struck by the plague. And on top of that, Marcus suffered various illnesses, as well as a betrayal by his wife Faustina. To cope with all the difficult people he faced on a daily basis, he lay the groundwork for a Stoic exercise called the 'negative visualization' that fortifies the mind by adjusting our expectations. The negative visualization, or *praemeditatio malorum*, is a Stoic exercise usually done in the morning in which one visualizes the possible difficulties, discomforts and adversities one could encounter during the day, as a means of preparation. My other book, *Stoicism for Inner Peace*, goes deeper into this exercise.

Marcus Aurelius kept a personal journal that, most likely, wasn't meant to be published. Yet, two millennia later, his thoughts are spreading across the internet and his journal, now known as *Meditations,* has gained fame as one of the most profound, surviving Stoic works. In the eleventh book of *Meditations*, Marcus encourages himself to live virtuously, without being stopped by the people that stand in his way. For not everyone wants the best for us, and some try to sabotage us. But, regardless of what they do, we can't blame them for our faults, as they're unable to affect our ability to choose. Thus, we are responsible for our own choices. Marcus wrote:

> *Someone despises me. That's their problem. Mine: not to do or say anything despicable. Someone hates me. Their problem. Mine: to be patient and cheerful with everyone, including them. Ready to show them their mistake. Not spitefully, or to show off my own self-control, but in an honest, upright way.*

Marcus Aurelius, *Meditations*, 11.13 (translated by Gregory Hays)

Marcus also emphasized the significance of understanding that adversity is a natural part of life and that how we choose to react to it determines our resilience. He wrote:

> *The art of living is more like wrestling than dancing, because an artful life requires being prepared to meet and withstand sudden and unexpected attacks.*

Marcus Aurelius, *Meditations*, 7.61 (translated by Gerald H. Rendall)

And also:

To be like the rock that the waves keep crashing over. It stands unmoved and the raging of the sea falls still around it.

Marcus Aurelius, *Meditations*, 4.49 (translated by Gregory Hays)

To conclude, Seneca advised us to let go of our ideals about how the world should be, and, instead, take it how it is. Also, he told us that we cannot live well if we don't know how to die well. Thus, we shouldn't close our eyes to misfortune; instead we should expect it, and see it as a part of life.

Epictetus told us that the things beyond our control are weak and slavish, so they're unreliable factors to hinge our happiness upon. It's better to be indifferent towards anything independent of our own will. These things are inferior to what's truly within our power: our own actions.

Chrysippus, the greatest of all Stoics, further developed the Stoic system of ethics, showing us that a happy life is a virtuous life. Courage (or fortitude) is one of the cardinal virtues, meaning that we must be willing to endure discomfort and face our fears, in order to live well. If we choose to engage in vices instead, we may experience short-term pleasure, but this will lead to unhappiness in the long run.

Marcus Aurelius wrote that no matter how severe the external circumstances are; they won't impede our ability to choose. Therefore, we can't blame other people for our faults. We are responsible for our own choices. The less we care about the things that don't matter, the stronger our determination will be.

If fortitude and mental toughness are desirable qualities to develop, how did the ancients view success?

Chapter 6 Success

Even though the Stoics are concerned with cultivating tranquility, the ultimate goal is to live virtuously and in harmony with nature. As such, there is a concept of 'success' within Stoicism, characterized by a life rich in virtue (see chapter 2: Virtues, Vices & Indifferents).

The writings of Marcus Aurelius provide numerous insights grounded in logic and reason that can help us develop a mindset conducive to success. Even though these insights focus mainly on virtue and ethical living, they can be interpreted and applied more broadly to personal development and individual pursuits.

In this piece, we will delve into five such teachings that can guide us on our path to personal and professional achievement.

(1) Creating your teachers

Marcus Aurelius drew lessons from many individuals in his immediate circle. It is truly inspiring to read how he identified positive qualities in people and sought to incorporate these lessons into his own life. For example, from his mother, he learned generosity; from his great-grandfather, he embraced the value of private education over public schools; from Diognetus (not to be confused with the Cynic philosopher Diogenes), he understood the importance of not wasting time on trivial matters; and from Maximus (his teacher), he acquired self-control.

Marcus regarded various people, ranging from close family members to the gods, as his teachers. For him, teachers were not limited to conventional educators but could be anyone. Rather than focusing on people's shortcomings, he concentrated on their positive traits that he could adopt in his own life. This approach can inspire us to do the same: we can observe those around us, and instead of dwelling on their flaws, we can admire and learn from their admirable qualities. Our sources of learning can extend to philosophers, celebrities, or even religious figures.

Moreover, even those we perceive as 'bad' or 'toxic' may possess traits we can admire and cultivate within ourselves. By transforming the people around us into teachers rather than competitors, enemies, or villains, we foster an environment of collaboration and mutual growth. Embracing this mindset ultimately increases our likelihood of achieving success.

(2) Not caring about them

While this may seem contradictory to the previous teaching, Marcus also emphasizes the importance of not being overly concerned with the opinions of others. He states:

The tranquility that comes when you stop caring what they say. Or think, or do. Only what you do. Not to be distracted by their darkness. To run straight for the finish line, unswerving.

Marcus Aurelius, *Meditations*, 4.18 (translated by Gregory Hays)

In many instances, we witness people holding each other back. For example, when I started my YouTube-channel, numerous people expressed skepticism, suggesting that I would be better off (and more secure) focusing on my regular job. In some respects, they were right; the conventional nine-to-five path often offers more stability. However, they spoke from their own perspective, which might be entirely different from mine. This doesn't mean that seeking advice from others is futile, but, ultimately, you are the best judge of what's right for you. The skeptics didn't share my vision or knowledge, so they couldn't envision my ideas the way I could. Even though I respected their opinions, I didn't let them deter me from pursuing my plans.

While some skeptics may have good intentions, others may harbor malicious motives and attempt to sabotage our progress. In such cases, Marcus Aurelius' guidance is invaluable: "Don't be distracted by their darkness." Many people are envious and derive pleasure from witnessing the failures of others. This often reflects their own insecurities and shortcomings, and may not have anything to do with us.

(3) Do what's essential

Now, another teaching by Marcus Aurelius can be seen as a form of minimalism. Many people, myself included, have fallen into the trap of doing many things that aren't relevant, thus wasting a lot of time and energy. When we don't have a clear image of what we have to do to reach our goals, we become aimless. The consequence is that we become stressed out, or even burned out. That's why it's important to stick with the essentials. Marcus Aurelius writes:

> *If you seek tranquility, do less. Or (more accurately) do what's essential—what the logos of a social being requires, and in the requisite way. Which brings a double satisfaction: to do less, better. Because most of what we say and do is not essential. If you can eliminate it, you'll have more time, and more tranquility. Ask yourself at every moment, "Is this necessary?" But we need to eliminate unnecessary assumptions as*

> *well to eliminate the unnecessary actions that follow.*
>
> Marcus Aurelius, *Meditations*, 4.24 (translated by Gregory Hays)

Prioritizing the essentials rarely fails us. If we desire more tranquility in life, we may want to focus on what's essential. If we aim to build a business, concentrating on the essentials and discarding everything irrelevant is an effective strategy. To keep myself on track, I make it a habit to write down the tasks for the upcoming day the night before. These tasks might include writing a script, shopping for groceries, or engaging in other meaningful activities—anything besides idling on the couch. This not only gives me focus but also provides clarity even before I go to bed. Knowing what I need to accomplish the next day helps me sleep better as well. It also prevents me from engaging in non-essential activities, as my tasks are clearly defined.

(4) Changing your perceptions

Hardship is an inevitable part of life. When we're trying to achieve something, we can expect resistance. Marcus Aurelius experienced many setbacks during his reign as emperor of Rome: lost battles, betrayal, and his wife, Faustina, cheating on him with Cassius, the governor of Syria, when he himself was sick. But like the

Stoic he was, Marcus Aurelius stayed grounded, accepting these events as part of nature and, thus, beyond his control. As stated earlier, whether or not we are harmed by hardship doesn't depend on the hardship itself, but on the way we look at it. It's a matter of perception. Marcus Aurelius wrote:

> *Choose not to be harmed—and you won't feel harmed. Don't feel harmed—and you haven't been.*

Marcus Aurelius, *Meditations*, 4.7 (translated by Gregory Hays)

Marcus' advice sounds a bit simplistic, but it's actually the basis of a popular and widely used method in psychology called *cognitive behavioral therapy* (CBT). This form of therapy is based on the idea that emotions are rooted in thought. Thus, a certain event isn't the root of how we feel, but our thoughts about this event are. If we, instead of aversion, develop neutrality towards the thing we perceive as undesirable, we don't feel harmed if it occurs. And if we don't feel harmed, we haven't been harmed, according to Marcus Aurelius' view, meaning that we don't arouse the passions in ourselves as a response to outside circumstances (see chapter 3: The Passions). Knowing this, makes us more resilient on our path to success because it's much easier to accept setbacks, and continue in spite of them.

(5) Following nature's way

Following nature's way means taking the shortest and easiest route, according to Marcus Aurelius. This idea seems similar to the Taoist concept of taking the path of least resistance. So, how do we follow nature's way in the Stoic sense?

> *Take the shortest route, the one that nature planned—to speak and act in the healthiest way. Do that, and be free of pain and stress, free of all calculation and pretension.*

Marcus Aurelius, *Meditations*, 4.51 (translated by Gregory Hays)

Well, I admit Marcus' advice is a bit vague. Although, considering the Stoic end goal, he might be advocating to living virtuously, so conformable to Stoic ethics. However, in the second book of *Meditations*, he tells us to consider the nature of the world, our own nature, and how we relate to the world, which shows a wider perspective on 'nature.' So, extrapolating from this broader view, we could ask ourselves:

- What are my strengths?
- What are my weaknesses?

- Which activities are most suitable for me?
- In what way can I contribute to the world that befits my own nature?
- Do I perform better alone or in teams?
- And so on.

By respecting our own nature, and just being who we are as humans and as individuals, we might discover the shortest and easiest route to success. There's no fixed set of criteria when it comes to following our own nature. We have to find out ourselves what's right for us.

There's an ideological and ethical side to this as well. From a Stoic perspective, our success must be a contribution to humanity. One can be a successful drug dealer, but from an ethical point of view, this person's success is tragic for humanity. And not only for humanity but for the people themselves as well, as this 'profession' goes hand-in-hand with great stress, calculation, pretension, and for the risk of violence in the name of greed.

Therefore, as a Stoic, it's essential to take into consideration the manner in which personal success benefits the world. If it harms the world, it isn't success. As Marcus states: "My city and state are Rome—as with Antoninus. But as a human being? The world. So for me, 'good' can only mean what's good for both communities."

If success is then characterized by a life rich in virtue, what could block our success? What happens when we face adversity?

Chapter 7   Calm in Uncertainty

The ancient Stoics did not shy away from adversity; instead, they persevered and continued on their paths of virtue. In times of profound uncertainty, the capacity to remain composed is therefore a rare commodity. A glimpse into the memoirs of Marcus Aurelius reveals his struggles to fulfill his duties without succumbing to the pressures of his position or indulging in sensual pleasures like so many other emperors, including his own son.

Fear is the birthplace of hatred and violence, hostility and oppression. As this emotion pervades the globe, infecting us all like a virus, our collective suffering intensifies. Here is where the potency of Stoicism resides, not in altering our circumstances, but in bolstering ourselves so that we can *face* our circumstances, regardless of their severity. Within Stoicism, we can discover the essential wisdom needed to cultivate greater resilience, not only to preserve our inner tranquility but also to flourish and radiate strength amidst times of uncertainty.

(1) It's not the events that disturb us

Stoics and Buddhists will agree that, in regards to the human experience, there's nothing that precedes the mind. Even though we feel it's the external world that upsets us, it's actually the way we think about the world that is to blame. It's true that outside circumstances may directly influence our ideas and presuppositions, or trigger what lies hidden in the subconscious mind, like deeply rooted beliefs or, perhaps, repressed experiences. But, it's still the mind that creates the experience. For example, we believe that we shouldn't face hardships like disease or financial setbacks. Or that we shouldn't suffer a loss, in whatever form that may be. Unfortunately, this means that we're still in denial of the reality of nature. Unpleasant events happen to all of us, and no one has the right to be excluded from the universal ways of change.

However, according to the Stoics, we do have a choice. The flow of life, the aging of our bodies, illness, war, disease, all these are not ours to control. But we *do* have agency in spite of this. We can form opinions, we can judge, we can act. For example, we can discard the opinion that only good should overtake us, and accept that even the most catastrophic events of humanity may very well appear on our path. From a Stoic point of view, this shouldn't be a source of fear, but an opportunity to accept reality, and stop resisting the inevitable. This sentiment alone leads to inner peace; it's a matter of embracing whatever happens, and knowing that not the events but our own experience is what causes how we feel.

(2) Most things have happened before

Like many creatures on Earth, we humans possess a limited perspective of the unfolding of life. To a large extent, this narrow view shapes our experience of the world. Consider the mayfly, a small insect that is born and dies the same day. This creature is unaware of night, seasons, years, or decades. Its vision of the world is extremely narrow, so that events it encounters as once-in-a-lifetime experiences are merely daily occurrences for us.

Consider how the universe reveals itself in cycles and waves. Unless we live through at least one cycle or wave, the events we encounter might seem unprecedented. However, upon examining history, we realize that most events that disturb and frighten us have already transpired before. They simply have not happened within our lifetime, so they appear as if they have never occurred before. Wars, pandemics, natural disasters, as well as conflicts between ethnic groups, and the tensions between conservative and progressive-minded people—these struggles often disrupt our inner peace. Yet, the archives of old newspapers reveal that these are archetypal expressions of all ages, repeating themselves time and again. As Marcus Aurelius observed:

> *Look at the past—empire succeeding empire—and from that, extrapolate the future: the same thing. No escape from the rhythm of events. Which is why observing*

life for forty years is as good as a thousand.
Would you really see anything new?

Marcus Aurelius, *Meditations*, 7.49 (translated by Gregory Hays)

(3) Our thoughts are unreliable

The mind is a powerful biological machine that's capable of turning fantasy into reality. Our ability to think is the reason why we survived in a world that's often hostile to us, as it's inhabited by many animals that are physically much stronger than we are. The mind has also created the most beautiful pieces of art, literature, architecture, and brought us to the moon, and eventually to other planets. Without a doubt, it's a powerful tool. But there are dangers too.

Exploring possible outcomes can be a good thing. But when we overdo it, we get stuck in the maelstrom of excessive thinking, which destroys our inner peace. We think about possible scenarios over and over again, often in ways that are irrational and based on assumption. We worry about the future, about all the terrible things that could happen. Sure, it's very well possible that our forebodings come to pass. But a thought, is just a thought. It's not real. The menu is not the meal. We can read the menu a thousand times, but it still doesn't compare to the food on our plate. Epictetus once said:

Men are disturbed not by things, but by the views which they take of things. Thus death is nothing terrible, else it would have appeared so to Socrates. But the terror consists in our notion of death, that it is terrible.

Epictetus, *Enchiridion*, 5 (translated by T.W. Higginson)

(4) Adversity can make us stronger

How terrible it is that we're going through so much misery, right? Well, Marcus Aurelius would have disagreed. After all, isn't it great when we're still alive and able to thrive after all we've been through? Stoicism isn't about avoiding life, but avoiding being mentally destroyed because of life happening. Without a doubt, this is easier said than done. But from a Stoic mindset, we shouldn't focus on how bad things are at the moment, but on how we get through them and maintain inner peace while doing so. Every minute we spend on feeling bad about our situation—and resisting what is—we could spend on making the best out of our lives regardless of what's happening to us.

For instance, the more headwinds we experience while cycling, the more we have to use our leg muscles, and the stronger they become. Therefore, when we see bad times as an opportunity to create strength, we might stop fearing them, and embrace them instead.

> *It's unfortunate that this has happened. No. It's fortunate that this has happened and I've remained unharmed by it—not shattered by the present or frightened of the future.*

Marcus Aurelius, *Meditations*, 4-49a (translated by Gregory Hays)

(5) Living in the present eases our burden

Compared to humans, animals seem to live much more in the immediate present. Seneca noticed how animals experience fear when there's danger, but after they escape it, they don't dwell on it anymore: they either go through flight or fight, or carry on living as if nothing happened afterward. We humans, on the other hand, can ruminate on past events for a lifetime, and camp in a state of perpetual worry until death liberates us. We let our memories bring back past hurts, we let worry torment us, while, in reality, there's nothing happening but our thoughts.

It's only when we stay in the present that we're free from worry and rumination. This doesn't mean that our memories are invalid, or that we should never anticipate or plan for the future, but that the past and future cannot touch us, because they do not exist. Stoicism underlines that the present is all we have. When we stick with the situation at hand, we'll have a lot less to worry about.

(6) Embracing life's impermanence

From the moment we're born, our life has been ticking away second after second. Death is an inevitable consequence of life. And, at the same time, it's the most destructive thing that can happen to us, as it's the disintegration and annihilation of what we perceive as ourselves. As Seneca stated:

> *For we are mistaken when we look forward to death; the major portion of death has already passed. Whatever years be behind us are in death's hands.*

Lucius Annaeus Seneca, *Moral Letters to Lucilius*, 1.2 (translated by Richard M. Gummere)

Life, therefore, is this amazing journey full of surprises. What a waste of time to spend our lives in anguish, and to resist everything we encounter, always busy creating this false sense of security while the very nature of the universe *is* insecurity! Spending this day worrying is kind of stupid, if we could die tomorrow. From a Stoic perspective, it makes more sense to spend our time well. if we remember that our time here is limited, it will loosen the grip of the past and future on us. So let us seize the day while maintaining inner peace!

(7) Embracing our insignificance within the grand scheme

If we're still overly occupied by anxiety, especially in times of uncertainty, putting our lives in perspective may help us. Remember the mayfly? From a human perspective, the life of the mayfly comes across as a rather insignificant blip on the screen. But for the 4,700 year old tree, Methuselah, the oldest tree in the world, a human life equals about a year. This tree is even older than all the ancient Stoics put together, and during its lifetime many human civilizations have come and gone. For Methuselah, the human lifespan doesn't amount to much.

Now, compare this to the history of our planet, and then put our planet in the timeframe of the cosmos: now we've been reduced to almost nothing! This doesn't mean that the human experience doesn't count; we're gifted with the ability to experience deeply, which is a beautiful thing, regardless of our size and lifespan. But by taking a Stoic view from above, we remind ourselves of how transient life actually is. That might make us realize that many of the small (and even big) things we're worrying about today will mean next to nothing, let's say, a hundred years from now.

Chapter 8   Suffering in Imagination

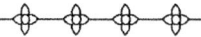

In the last chapter we talked about worrying about things in the future that might or might not happen. How pointless it is! Let's look into the concept of worry and why it is so detrimental.

In a letter to his dear friend Lucilius Stoic philosopher Seneca wrote:

> *There are more things, Lucilius, likely to frighten us than there are to crush us; we suffer more often in imagination than in reality.*

Lucius Annaeus Seneca, *Moral Letters to Lucilius*, 13.4 (translated by Richard M. Gummere)

Chronic worriers often find themselves preoccupied with the future rather than the present circumstances. Throughout the day, and even the night, their thoughts wander through the mysterious realm of what's yet to come, plotting, planning, and calculating how to tackle an unfortunate fate that may not even emerge. However, despite their desire to control the future, they have never ventured beyond the confines of the present. This is because the future does not exist, except in our minds. We cannot live in the future, nor can we predict it.

Nevertheless, many of us fixate on the unknown, endlessly fantasizing about how things that we cannot possibly predict will manifest themselves. Seneca observed this phenomenon in his friend Lucilius and the people around him. He challenged this often tiresome and destructive stance towards the future with Stoic reasoning, elucidating why worrying about it is futile, and advising us what to do instead.

This chapter delves into antidotes to worry and unfounded fears, offering insights to help us overcome our preoccupation with the uncertainties of the future. We'll start with Seneca's letter to Lucilius named *Groundless Fears,* and then look at Marcus Aurelius' writings and Epictetus' sayings.

(1) Identify groundless fears

The notion that the future doesn't exist doesn't negate the passage of time. It doesn't deny that the present moment will soon become the past, and that we are perpetually confronted with a stream of novelty, much like a mountaintop facing a relentless and unpredictable blizzard. The mountain cannot anticipate what's coming; it can only endure and observe the snowflakes as they whizz by, just as we watch moments pass, transitioning from, what we call the future, to the past. We know that something is coming, but, regardless of how we attempt to interpret it or how well we prepare for it, we'll always be shooting in the dark. Ultimately, the future we imagine lacks a solid foundation as it consists of nothing more than ideas ranging from wild guesses to statistical projections. Despite this, many people are burdened by these ideas, leading them to suffer from groundless fears rooted in speculation rather than truth. As Seneca observed:

> *For truth has its own definite boundaries, but that which arises from uncertainty is delivered over to guesswork and the irresponsible license of a frightened mind.*

Lucius Annaeus Seneca, *Moral Letters to Lucilius*, 13.9 (translated by Richard M. Gummere)

Seneca noted that some things affect us before they even materialize, while others fill us with foreboding when, in reality, they never will. This occurs because we are habitually "exaggerating, or imagining, or anticipating sorrow." In his letter, Seneca elaborates on the nature of the mind, explaining to Lucilius that it sometimes conjures false images of evil when no evil is present. As he puts it:

> *It twists into the worst construction some word of doubtful meaning; or it fancies some personal grudge to be more serious than it really is, considering not how angry the*

> *enemy is, but to what lengths he may go if he is angry.*

Lucius Annaeus Seneca, *Moral Letters to Lucilius*, 13.12 (translated by Richard M. Gummere)

This human tendency to worry is not only unpleasant but can also be detrimental to our well-being. Ample scientific evidence suggests that worrying can cause physical and mental illness. This means that, even though the future doesn't exist, we are worrying ourselves sick over it. Fortunately, Seneca's writings offer us remedies for these groundless fears.

(2) Are Your Sufferings Real or Imaginary?

What antidotes did Seneca suggest for combating the human habit of worrying? His remedy revolves around fortifying the mind with certain ideas and truths about reality, as well as altering our attitude towards fortune and misfortune. Firstly, he reminds his friend Lucilius that, although many unfortunate events have befallen him, he has always managed to hold his ground. Somehow, he is always able to cope. Examining the history of our own lives, we may find that, what we perceive in advance as a catastrophe often turns out differently than we imagined; frequently, we suffer less than we anticipated; ironically, most of the suffering occurs before the actual event takes place.

Consider the anxiety surrounding an exam. In the weeks leading up to it, we worry daily: "Will I have a mental block? Will I mess up?" However, the anxiety experienced during the exam is negligible compared to the preceding weeks. The root of this fear lies in our beliefs about the consequences of failing the exam. We might think, "If I fail, my life is over," or "If I don't pass this exam, then it's true what they say: I am indeed a failure." Even though some catastrophic beliefs about the future may be plausible, as long as they're not manifesting at this very moment, what is there to be disturbed about? As Seneca noted:

> *You may retort with the question: "How am I to know whether my sufferings are real or imaginary?" Here is the rule for such matters: We are tormented either by things present, or by things to come, or by both. As to things present, the decision is easy. Suppose that your person enjoys freedom and health and that you do not suffer from any external injury. As to what may happen to it in the future, we shall see later on. Today there is nothing wrong with it.*

Lucius Annaeus Seneca, *Moral Letters to Lucilius*, 13.7 (translated by Richard M. Gummere)

In the same letter, Seneca encourages Lucilius to be cautious about external influences when it comes to his personal situation. It is better to trust ourselves and independently consult our feelings, as we know our affairs better than anyone else. Why should we be easily influenced by the opinions and views of other people, many of whom are only too eager to plant seeds of fear in our minds? And so Seneca urges Lucilius to consult reason to determine whether he is not transforming "what is not an evil into what is an evil." The antidote, then, is to carefully distinguish between imagination and reality. As soon as we realize that our fears are based on irrational thoughts, fantasies, or exaggerations, our worries are debunked.

(3) Exercise prudence in your thought life

The act of worrying can be viewed as a form of indulgence. Worriers wallow in their many thoughts about the future, all of them stories created by themselves. Like our favorite television show or video game, we choose to entertain ourselves with these fantasies and keep them coming to occupy our minds. But, according to Seneca, doing so is not a good way to live. He argued that many times, the mind creates false shapes out of what our senses perceive, making reality worse than it is:

> *The mind at times fashions for itself false shapes of evil when there are no signs that point to any evil.*

Lucius Annaeus Seneca, *Moral Letters to Lucilius*, 13.12 (translated by Richard M. Gummere)

These fantasies may seem useful, as we believe we can use them for anticipating the future. But by occupying our minds with all these imaginations and speculations, we might cause unnecessary suffering for ourselves and others. Panic is contagious. And so, if we spread doom and gloom, others will follow suit.

For instance, envision a group of men advancing in the distance. We don't know these individuals, their origins, or their intentions. The sight of these men incites our imagination to run wild: they're out to get us, they're probably going to kidnap us, beat us, and torture us. As we stand there, hands shaking, legs trembling, and sweat streaming down our faces, we declare to others that our lives are over—a wave of panic ensues. However, in due course, these 'menacing' figures simply stroll past us, some even offering greetings. So, the crux of the matter is no disaster occurred.

More often than not, our fantasies about the future will not come to fruition. They don't exist outside of our minds. Yet, many people spend every waking hour creating and entertaining these fantasies. But, as Seneca stated:

> *..life is not worth living, and there is no limit to our sorrows, if we indulge our fears to the greatest possible extent; in this matter, let prudence help you, and contemn with a resolute spirit even when it is in plain sight.*

Lucius Annaeus Seneca, *Moral Letters to Lucilius*, 13.12 (translated by Richard M. Gummere)

So, Seneca offers us a solution to buttress ourselves against imagining catastrophes: just be *prudent*. In this context, he points to being *mindful* of our fantasies and keeping them at bay as much as possible. So, even when there's a clear sign that a threat should come to pass, we should still be prudent in regard to our thoughts about it. Prudence is a form of self-control in the way we engage in our thoughts. Acquiring prudence takes practice.

(4) Even Bad Fortune is Fickle

Another antidote Seneca proposes involves a shift in attitude towards future events. Seneca urged Lucilius, not to jump to conclusions too quickly regarding the nature of what Fortuna, the goddess of chance, luck and fate, provides. Considering our human ignorance about not only how events will unfold, but also the nature of these events and their precise impact on our lives, it's wise to exercise caution when judging fate. In some cases, the 'misfortune' we anticipate indeed materializes. However, events can sometimes take such an unexpected turn that, against all odds, we escape unscathed.

This can be seen in a Buddhist story about a man pursued by a tiger. The man jumps into an old well and encounters a snake at the bottom. He clings tightly to a root protruding from the wall, which is being gnawed on by mice. His fate appears sealed, but then, out of the blue, Fortuna presents him with an escape. The tiger, in his eagerness to paw the man, loses his balance and tumbles into the well. It lands on the snake crushing it to death. The impact kills the tiger as well. The man manages to pull himself out unscathed.

Thus, adversity can strike at any time, but so can a stroke of luck amidst terrible circumstances. "Even bad fortune is fickle," Seneca asserted. His antidote is to maintain an open mind about the future, recognizing that we cannot judge the nature of an event before it has happened and its consequences are revealed. He wrote:

> *Let us, then, look carefully into the matter. It is likely that some troubles will befall us, but it is not a present fact. How often has the unexpected happened! How often has the expected never come to pass! And even though it is ordained to be, what does it avail to run out to meet your suffering? You will*

suffer soon enough when it arrives; so look forward meanwhile to better things.

Lucius Annaeus Seneca, *Moral Letters to Lucilius*, 13.10 (translated by Richard M. Gummere)

This does not mean we should deny that bad things might happen. Seneca does not encourage his friend to ignore the potential for severe outcomes. Instead, he advocates careful observation: it's unwise to deny misfortune, but we also shouldn't let the slightest hint of adversity send us reeling into a panic. The key is finding the middle path between ignorance and obsession, mindfully assessing the situation while keeping all options open.

(5) Don't be a cowardly scout

In his *Discourses*, Epictetus recounts the tale of a timorous scout dispatched to Rome who returned terror-stricken. The scout described Rome as a fearful place where death, exile, and poverty lurked at every corner, claiming that all these things were "terrible," and that the enemy was upon them. But when Diogenes was sent to Rome as a scout, he returned with a different report. He did not deny what the other scout had seen: there was indeed death, exile, and poverty. But instead of being in a panic about these things, he said:

Death is not evil since it is not dishonorable. To sleep on the bare ground is the softest couch. There's no enemy near. All is full of peace.

Diogenes (as told by Epictetus), *Discourses*, 1.24 (translated by W.A. Oldfather)

When Diogenes was asked why he thought that no enemy was near, he simply replied:

I have not been struck with any missile, have I, or received any wound? I have not fled from anyone, have I?

Diogenes (as told by Epictetus), *Discourses*, 1.24 (translated by W.A. Oldfather)

The scout was paralyzed by fear over the sights in Rome; hence in his mind, the enemy had already arrived. However, Diogenes perceived none of what he saw as a threat or "terrifying," and thus found no reason to worry. Unsurprisingly, the Stoics would argue that Diogenes' interpretation of Rome's situation was more accurate. There was no impending enemy. Death, exile, and poverty weren't "terrifying." Since these elements didn't interfere with virtue, they were simply dismissed as 'indifferents' neither good nor bad and incapable of enhancing or diminishing the quality of a joyful life (see chapter 2: Virtues, Vices & Indifferents). So, the antidote here is to see things clearly and assess whether or not they're actually worth worrying about.

(6) Don't be beggarly

According to ancient Stoics, Zeus, the king of gods, governs our fates, and no amount of contemplation or worry can change that. Whatever Zeus does, desires, or decides, the fact remains it is beyond our control. At times, his whims may be as unpredictable as the Dutch weather. Fortunately, Zeus bestowed upon us mortals a precious gift: the power to choose. We may not have the power to resist his rule, but we can decide how we react to what he throws at us, no matter how bleak.

The following passage from Marcus Aurelius' *Meditations* presents us with two ways to approach the future: focusing nobly on the things up to us or pleading with the gods to make things happen (or not happen), like beggars.

> *Either the gods have power or they don't. If they don't, why pray? If they do, then why not pray for something else instead of for things to happen or not to happen? Pray not to feel fear. Or desire, or grief. If the gods can do anything, they can surely do that for us. - But those are things the gods left up to me. Then isn't it better to do what's up to you*

> *- like a free man - than to be passively controlled by what isn't, like a slave or beggar? And what makes you think the gods don't care about what's up to us?"*

Marcus Aurelius, *Meditations*, 9.40 (translated by Gregory Hays)

Humanity, by and large, has tethered its mental states to outside circumstances. And so, we often spend our days searching for external sources of happiness and avoiding external sources of pain. But by doing so, our suffering will be endless, as the external world is unreliable. And so we worry: will Fate grant our wishes or not? Will the gods spare us from misfortune or not? The only solution is to wish for *exactly* what is within our control.

> *But, if you wish to have your desires undisappointed, this is in your own control. Exercise, therefore, what is in your control. He is the master of every other person who is able to confer or remove whatever that person wishes either to have or to avoid. Whoever, then, would be free, let him wish nothing, let him decline nothing, which depends on others, else he must necessarily be a slave.*

Epictetus, *Enchiridion*, 14 (translated by Elizabeth Carter)

In the final analysis, if our contentment does not depend on external circumstances, we're truly free. Nothing that happens will disturb us. And so, if we embrace anything the future provides us with, what's left to worry about?

Chapter 9   Not Clinging

When we cling to the fickle and unreliable outside world, our very sense of wellbeing is held hostage. Around two thousand years ago, Stoic philosopher Epictetus observed that people were burdened and weighed down because they tended to care about too many things. His remedy, however, is not to cease caring altogether, but to care about the right things and stop clinging to anything insignificant.

According to Epictetus, what matters and what doesn't is determined by the reality of our place as rational beings in an ever-changing environment. He makes this clear in the underlying tenet of his work: 'the dichotomy of control.' Some things are within our control, while others are not. By concerning ourselves with what we can control, we position ourselves for strength. Conversely, if we neglect these things and focus on what's beyond our control, we place ourselves in a position of weakness. Clinging on to what's not up to us sets the stage for a life of suffering. But what are those things we cling to, and why is it better to let them go?

The two primary sources of Epictetus' philosophy, *Discourses* and *Enchiridion*, offer insights on attaining contentment and inner peace. This includes fortifying our minds against external circumstances that would typically cause us distress. In the first chapter of

Discourses, Epictetus clarifies that external circumstances can only hurt us if we let them—that is, if we cling to them. He cites the example of going into exile, stating that being exiled wouldn't prevent him from departing with a smile or remaining cheerful and serene. If he had clung to the notion that exile was a great tragedy or that the possessions and people he was separated from was the end of life, he would have been in agony. Epictetus understood that the choice to be cheerful and serene is ours, while the possibility of exile is not. Thus, he disregarded the former and concentrated on the latter. By focusing solely on what we can control and releasing everything else, nothing outside of ourselves can harm us.

The question then arises: what exactly is within our control, and what isn't? Epictetus explains this in the first chapter of the Enchiridion:

> *Some things are in our control and others not. Things in our control are opinion, pursuit, desire, aversion, and, in a word, whatever are our own actions. Things not in our control are body, property, reputation, command, and, in one word, whatever are not our own actions.*

Epictetus, *Enchiridion*, 1 (translated by Elizabeth Carter)

In essence, the external world is beyond our control, but the way we choose to act and position ourselves within it is. Epictetus does not encourage us to become indifferent to everything. On the contrary, living a good and moral life in accordance with nature is a Stoic's primary objective, which is entirely within our control. However, he does urge us not to cling to what is not within our control because these things are capricious, fragile, and unreliable.

The enchanting, exciting outside world of pleasure—sweet but insatiable—often entices us to pursue it. Consequently, we desire what the world has to offer and cling to anything that delights the mind and senses. Unfortunately, the loss of what we cling to is painful. What we gain and lose is subject to Fate. If our happiness relies on things beyond our control, then, from a Stoic viewpoint, we've subjected our emotions to the whims of Fortuna. Thus, it is crucial that we cease clinging to matters beyond our control if we want to develop a strong and stable sense of well-being. Fortunately, Epictetus provides us with situations and methods to achieve this, emphasizing the power of our reasoning mind and devaluing the things outside of it.

(1) Not clinging to objects, people, and power

Inherent in human nature is the tendency to form attachments, not only to the people but also to objects we like. As a result, we revel in the presence of those we care for, and are tormented when they depart from our lives. More tragically, we sometimes suffer the loss of a loved one even before it happens, as it unfolds in our imagination. Clinging to someone or something signifies the perpetual pain that accompanies resistance to a possible, yet ultimately inevitable, separation from the object of our attachment. In some instances, the fear of loss or abandonment escalates into an obsession, causing our entire lives to center on preventing separation.

The same principle applies to power. As the ancient Greek philosopher Epicurus noted, the quest for power is insatiable—thus, obtaining power frequently incites an unquenchable thirst for more. How many times in history have we seen individuals corrupted by power inflict misery upon others, simply because they refused to relinquish their power and craved for more! Paradoxically, despite power's ostensible control, it is inherently beyond our control, as it can be granted or revoked at an instant.

Again, battling the impermanent nature of existence is futile. To live in accordance with nature, as the Stoics strive to do, we must adapt to life's transitory nature. But how? Epictetus offered a simple yet profound piece of advice for approaching the world in relation to objects, people, and power. How about treating life as a dinner party?

> *Is anything brought around to you? Put out your hand and take your share with moderation. Does it pass by you? Don't stop it. Is it not yet come? Don't stretch your desire towards it, but wait until it reaches you. Do this with regard to children, to a wife, to public posts, to riches, and you will eventually be a worthy partner of the feasts of the gods.*
>
> Epictetus, *Enchiridion*, 15 (translated by Elizabeth Carter)

He continued by stating that when we can get to the point of rejecting the offerings set before us, we'll not only be a partner at the feasts of the gods but also a partaker in their dominion. This idea highlights the importance of living in harmony with nature—or simply, "by how things are"—rather than in opposition to it. Epictetus sought to strengthen our resilience against the pain of loss by altering our perception of the things we cherish. Instead of believing that we own something or that we're entitled to something or someone, we could consider everything we possess as "borrowed":

> *Never say of anything, "I have lost it;" but, "I have returned it." Is your child dead? It is returned. Is your wife dead? She is returned. Is your estate taken away? Well, and is not that likewise returned? "But he*

> *who took it away is a bad man." What difference is it to you who the giver assigns to take it back? While he gives it to you to possess, take care of it; but don't view it as your own, just as travelers view a hotel.*

Epictetus, *Enchiridion*, 11 (translated by Elizabeth Carter)

When we think about it, Epictetus' perspective aligns closely with reality. We possess nothing truly, except the rational decision making part of our minds (hêgemonikon); if we genuinely owned our children, spouses, or estates, we could never lose them. As such, the notion of 'borrowing' better reflects the truth, since there will always come a time to return what isn't ours. Holding onto borrowed goods only invites suffering. According to Epictetus, possessing and even enjoying things is acceptable as long as we're willing and able to release them when the time comes. By adopting this mindset, we can live more harmoniously with the ephemeral nature of life, and cultivate a sense of inner peace, regardless of the shifting tides around us.

(2) Not clinging to others' opinions

It's remarkable how much we concern ourselves with the opinions of others. Countless individuals strive to be liked. But why? In today's world, not being liked rarely poses a threat to our survival, unlike tribal times when acceptance by the tribe was a matter of life and death. While garnering positive opinions can be advantageous, such as making friends, finding a romantic partner, or securing a job, Epictetus argues that these external factors are less important than our equanimity.

Epictetus tells us, for example, that we shouldn't be grieved when we aren't invited to a party, especially if we don't particularly like the host. Getting invited to a party comes at a cost, which is your attendance and praise. If we're not willing to invest time and energy in socializing with a particular person, we shouldn't be surprised if we don't get invited to their party. We can't have it both ways. By not getting invited, we may not experience the fun of that party, but we do have this, and I quote: "the not praising him, whom you don't like to praise; the not bearing with his behavior at coming in." Now, that sounds like a pretty good deal, doesn't it?

Regardless of the pleasure that it brings, the ongoing pursuit of being liked is, in fact, exhausting. Imagine praising people we don't want to praise, or attending social gatherings that we don't want to attend. And for what purpose? Not for the sake of tranquility, which cannot be achieved if we always worry about what people think? Furthermore, Epictetus said that we might be laughed at, ridiculed, and despised if that's the price we pay for "equanimity, freedom, and tranquility."

No, we must be content to be thought stupid, and so, when someone speaks ill of us, we can say: "He does not know my other faults, or else he would not have mentioned only these." At the end of the day, the opinions of other people are beyond our control, but the degree to which they affect us lies within our control. Do we cling to people's opinions and let ourselves be guided by them? Or do we take what benefit we can from them before we let them go to forever rot in the past? It all comes down to skillfully handling the tool we're given, which is our ability to form opinions about opinions. Thus Epictetus reminds us:

> *Remember, that not he who gives ill language or a blow insults, but the principle which represents these things as insulting. When, therefore, anyone provokes you, be assured that it is your own opinion which provokes you.*

Epictetus, *Enchiridion*, 20 (translated by Elizabeth Carter)

(3) Not clinging to outcomes and ideas

The universe sometimes subjects us to hardship without mercy. Try to control it, and we lose every time. Try to change what is, and we fight a battle we can't win. Yet, people are often preoccupied with what should happen now, what should have happened in the past, and what should happen in the future. And the more they resist, the more life will hurt. Epictetus tells us to treat people the way we should treat a servant. Even though a servant is expected to be obedient, he can make it clear that he's of such importance to us that it should be in his power to not always conform to that role.

People are people, and it's in their nature to not always behave as we wish. Now, what's more important: that a servant is never bad, or that the master is happy? We can't have it both ways. Accepting the fact that a servant doesn't always act as we please is the price we pay for equanimity. We can use this example as a metaphor for anything. For example, we can't expect the world to be inoffensive. Silencing people who are (in some people's eyes) offensive is not going to change the fact that there will always be someone offending someone as long as we haven't given up our humanity.

So, the idea of an inoffensive world in which humans are involved is unrealistic. And imposing such an ideal on others probably does more harm than good. A more useful approach would be to start with being kinder ourselves, which is something we have control over. Others may or may not follow our lead, but that is not up to us. As Epictetus stated:

> *Don't demand that things happen as you wish, but wish that they happen as they do happen, and you will go on well.*

Epictetus, *Enchiridion*, 8 (translated by Elizabeth Carter)

Epictetus continually emphasizes that while we can't control the world, we can control our attitude towards it. Someone can insult us, but can't control what we think or feel about this. Someone can take away our possessions or steal our money, but can't control whether or not we're depressed about it. Our business partner can cheat on us, but it's up to us to decide to what degree this will affect us and how we want to react. The comings and goings of people aren't up to us. If we nonetheless cling to them, we lose. But if we accept them, and focus on living well despite the whims of fortune, we win.

However, "winning" from a Stoic viewpoint may be perceived as "losing" from a societal perspective. When we don't cling to things like accumulating material possessions, external achievements, and admiration from others, we might fall into the loser category.

Chapter 10 Being a Loser

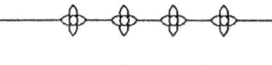

So the world sees us as losers because we don't meet society's expectations. But is that such a bad thing? It all depends on your perspective of winning and losing.

Epictetus offered valuable insights about the pursuits that society typically deems as markers of success, such as wealth and fame. He considered these achievements insignificant compared to the true treasures found within ourselves. Epictetus believed that the relentless pursuit of external validation prevents us from attaining a far superior prize: a blissful state, unshaken by the whims of the unpredictable external world, including the opinions of others.

You see, our fear of being perceived as losers often leads us to endure suffering in exchange for other people's approval. It's a disheartening existence, as by placing our bet on external goods, we become dependent on them and forfeit our chances of attaining true happiness and freedom. According to Epictetus, we must be willing to let go of what he called the "lesser things." And if that means becoming total losers in society's eyes, then it's a price worth paying. He does not advocate self-neglect or self-harm; quite the contrary, from a Stoic perspective. Epictetus, presents an alternative way to determine what's truly important in life. Once that is in place, the concept of "being a loser," and why being perceived as a loser doesn't have to be such a negative thing.

The anatomy of loserdom

Objectively, what is a loser? The Merriam-Webster dictionary offers a definition that aligns with the subject of this chapter: *a person who is incompetent or unable to succeed.*

But aren't competence and success subjective? When is someone competent? Some people might regard a certain person as competent, while others view that same individual as incompetent. The same goes for success. When is someone successful? For many, establishing and operating a small business like a hair salon is a success, while others might consider success as something outstanding like sending people to another planet. The definitions of competence and success are ever-changing, influenced by our zeitgeist, social atmosphere, demographics, culture, and religion. Consequently, the concept of being a "loser" is fluid, vague, and essentially reflects nothing more than the opinions of others.

However, if we place the notion of "loserdom" within the context of today's consumerist, capitalist society, we observe that it's deeply tied to the acquisition of external things, particularly money and fame. People often have a specific overall picture of what they need to feel complete, which varies widely. For many, it includes a well-paying job, an attractive partner, 2.3 children, and a white picket fence. For others, this vision may entail having a large social media following and an extensive, fascinating social circle that serves as evidence of their desirability. What if you don't conform to this overall picture? Then you're a loser—deemed incompetent at obtaining what's generally desired and, thus, incapable of succeeding in life.

Sadly, being labeled a loser is a double-edged sword. It signifies not only failure in others' eyes but also ridicule. But how desirable is it to possess what we're supposed to have in the first place? And how detrimental is it to be ridiculed if we don't have it? This is where Epictetus steps in.

Sacrificing for the overrated

What is the underlying need? What makes material possessions, extreme wealth, or Instagram fame so enticing? In essence, it's the promise of happiness that drives us to pursue all these externals. We fantasize about a world where throngs of people adore us as we enjoy cocktails on the beach, accumulating comments and likes on our social media pages. How marvelous this must feel! And, for a while, such a life may be splendid, but eventually, we'll adapt to it and revert to our baseline happiness, which now carries a heftier price tag.

Epictetus did not esteem these external goods highly. He characterized them as feeble, "slavish," and, most crucially, "beyond our control." By chasing after wealth and fame, we seek the unreliable, as we pursue what can vanish in an instant. Moreover, the quest for these things comes at a substantial cost: a price many are willing to pay, though they sacrifice much in the process. For instance, he cites someone who aspires to "conquer at the Olympic games," a pursuit that, if successful, garners considerable respect even today. However, he also encourages us to contemplate the sacrifices we must make, and to assess whether these truly benefit us.

> *You must conform to rules, submit to a diet, refrain from dainties; exercise your body, whether you choose it or not, at a stated hour, in heat and cold; you must drink no cold water, nor sometimes even wine. In a word, you must give yourself up to your master, as to a physician. Then, in the combat, you may be thrown into a ditch, dislocate your arm, turn your ankle, swallow dust, be whipped, and, after all, lose the victory.*

Epictetus, *Enchiridion*, 29 (translated by Elizabeth Carter)

So, is this worth it? Is it wise to go through such toil, just for, as Marcus Aurelius put it, "a clacking of tongues"? Especially if we think public praise is *fickle* and can change into public shame in the blink of an eye? "These things are not consistent," said Epictetus. He emphasized that only things *within our control* are worth pursuing, which are inner qualities like contentment, joy, right action, tranquility, and the power of restraint. The rest is overrated and belongs on the backburner.

Epictetus consistently distinguishes between the true nature of things and the mental representations we have of them. For instance, he observes that there is a difference between how we perceive our loved ones and their true essence. Although a man regards his wife and children as unique and more desirable than all other spouses and offspring, they are still human beings like everyone else. It is their appearance in our minds that makes them special to us, not their intrinsic qualities, independent of our judgment. We can apply this reasoning to all external matters. What renders the object we chase so alluring? Is it the object itself? Or is it our perception of that object?

But often, and unsurprisingly, we tend to be a flock of sheep desiring what others desire simply because everyone else does. Conversely, we don't want what nobody else wants, such as being considered a loser. It is not inherently wrong to want what others want. In many instances, what the majority pursues can be beneficial for health and well-being. However, in numerous other cases, it is not.

For example, in many European nations, alcohol is an integral part of social life. And if you don't drink on certain social occasions, you'll have some explaining to do. The majority of people pursue the buzz of alcohol, even though it has been scientifically proven that alcohol is bad for one's health. Another example is the relentless chase of social status and material goods, which is in itself could harmful (not always) as people tend to spend beyond their means, accumulate debt, and neglect more meaningful aspects of life, such as relationships and personal growth. And the constant chase could be harmful to one's health as well.

It takes wisdom and common sense to determine whether we are better off not chasing what everyone else seeks. Epictetus prioritized a state of happiness and freedom above all else, asserting that we should be willing to relinquish anything that hinders it. If that means being perceived as losers by others, then so be it.

Why being a loser isn't that terrible

What's so terrible about being seen as a "loser" anyway? Is it genuinely an unfortunate fate? Or do we perceive it as such because others make it to be so? Let's say we have enough to meet our basic needs, but not much else is happening in our lives. We don't have fascinating social circles, partners, social media followers, or exceptional jobs. As a result, people label us as losers, insinuating that we are somehow inferior to those making these judgments. Being seen as 'less' by others scares people because it directly attacks their egos: the narratives they create about themselves.

But is one truly less because they lack certain external trappings? Is someone wealthy and famous better than someone poor and unknown? According to Epictetus' logic, such reasoning is quite nonsensical.

> *These reasonings are unconnected: "I am richer than you, therefore I am better;" "I am more eloquent than you, therefore I am better." The connection is rather this: "I am richer than you, therefore my property is greater than yours;" "I am more eloquent than you, therefore my style is better than yours." But you, after all, are neither property nor style.*
>
> Epictetus, *Enchiridion*, 44 (translated by Elizabeth Carter)

Our external circumstances don't reveal much about our inner well-being, which is the truly significant entity from a Stoic perspective. However, we find them very important, so much so that we're willing to sacrifice our happiness and freedom to be regarded as 'sufficient' and not as 'less' by the masses. So, again, being a loser isn't inherently bad. It's what we make of it. If we view things like public praise, reputation, and others' opinions for what they are—namely, fickle, unreliable, often worthless, based on delusion and false appearances, and entirely beyond our control—we may find it easier to become indifferent to them. Then, we'll realize that being a loser is not that terrible. Being a loser doesn't hinder our ability to be happy and free; it's striving so hard not to be that does.

> *Let death and exile, and all other things which appear terrible, be daily before your eyes, but death chiefly; and you will never entertain any abject thought, nor too eagerly covet anything.*

Epictetus, *Enchiridion*, 21 (translated by T.W. Higginson)

A price worth paying

No matter which direction we decide to go, we'll have to pay some form of price. The question is: what price are we willing to pay? Epictetus makes a clear distinction between two options: "Be either a philosopher or one of the vulgar." Being vulgar (or 'commonplace,' the option most people choose) comes with a cost: our inner well-being. We pay the price required to attain what's considered desirable, like wealth and praise, meaning that we exchange our freedom, health, and inner peace to participate in the rat race and to keep up with the Joneses.

According to Epictetus, Being a philosopher means that we pay the price of probably not having, or at least, not pursuing, what the vulgar want. Hence, a Stoic may choose to live a very sober, obscure, simplistic lifestyle, devoid of external pleasure—in the eyes of many, as the archetypal loser—if that's what leads him or her down the road of living in agreement with nature. Although human beings are naturally inclined to survival and acquiring so-called 'preferred indifferents,' (see chapter 2: Virtues, Vices & Indifferents) a true philosopher, in Epictetus' view, always puts inner peace and happiness above things like money, status, and even hunger.

> *If you want to improve, reject such reasonings as these: "If I neglect my affairs, I'll have no income; if I don't correct my servant, he will be bad." For it is better to die with hunger, exempt from grief and fear, than to live in affluence with perturbation; and it is better your servant should be bad, than you unhappy.*
>
> Epictetus, *Enchiridion*, 12 (translated by Elizabeth Carter)

Though this may sound a tad extreme, Epictetus is at least consistent in prioritizing what he thinks is genuinely valuable. To be unconquerable by anything, we must be willing to lose everything. Anything external we hold onto, even the most minor thing, automatically wields power over our mental state. Leaving all this behind is a tough road, with many obstacles, little external recompense, and even loss and resistance.

> *You'll have to forego your ease, work hard, leave people behind, be despised by menials, be laughed at, and get crumbs at best when it comes to recognition and position—in all affairs. Consider these costs, and see if you're willing to pay them to gain peace, freedom and tranquility. If you're not willing, stay away from philosophy.*

Epictetus, *Enchiridion*, 29 (translated by Stephen Walton)

So, you're a loser in other people's eyes? Are you laughed at and even despised? At first sight, this might seem a terrible thing. The reputation of being a loser appears to be a weak and pitiful position. But it also has its advantages, namely, that we don't conform to other people's rules, and thus preserve the energy that we would've otherwise spent on what Epictetus called "lesser things," just to be seen as sufficient. In short, being a loser comes with the benefit of 'not paying the price for not being one.' And, ironically, that could make a loser a winner.

Drawing from Epictetus' words, one must have the wisdom to decide what's genuinely beneficial and the strength to stick with that consistently. One needs to have a healthy disregard for things like praise, riches, power, and social standing. As he stated: "(...) don't wish to be a general, or a senator, or a consul, but to be free; and the only way to this is a contempt of things not in our own control."

And, once you have arrived at the happy state of not minding being a loser, you are on the way to becoming unconquerable.

Chapter 11 Unconquerable

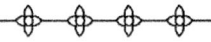

What does it mean to feel conquered? Does it happen when your country is overtaken by another? When an enemy seizes your home and belongings? When you're imprisoned, bound by your hands and feet? Or perhaps when someone steals your chance at love? The extent to which circumstances evoke a sense of defeat varies for each of us.

> *Bound upon me, rush upon me, I will overcome you by enduring your onset: whatever strikes against that which is firm and unconquerable merely injures itself by its own violence. Wherefore, seek some soft and yielding object to pierce with your darts.*
>
> Lucius Annaeus Seneca, *Of a Happy Life*, Book 27

The ancient Stoics offered a wealth of wisdom on how to become unconquerable. They believed that people cannot be conquered by anything external, as long as they don't give away their control over their faculties. The only way external things can influence us is when we ourselves let them. If we feel that something has vanquished us, it is actually our own selves succumbing to it. To become unconquerable, we need not triumph over the world, but rather, ourselves.

Emotionally conquered

How we perceive external factors determines their influence on us, not the factors themselves. If we assign great value to something, we risk developing a desire for it. When we encounter what we desire, we feel elated—a wonderful feeling. However, when we cannot attain what we want, our emotional state plummets. In doing so, we place our emotions at the mercy of external circumstances.

What if you develop a strong attraction for someone at work or school? If you successfully approach and secure a date with that person, you'll be on cloud nine. But if they cancel last minute, disappointment and frustration may follow. Though experiences like flaking, rejection, or breakups are common in dating, people's responses vary widely. Some effortlessly move on, while others harbor resentment and seek revenge. If rejection triggers a powerful emotional response, one could argue that the event has conquered us. It gains the power to influence our emotions and, potentially, our actions. This also applies to insults. When petty remarks breed days of resentment, the insulter has effectively conquered the insulted.

Facing tyrants

However, there are far more severe ways in which we allow others to conquer us than insults or rejection. For instance, manipulation through blackmail is one example. A common form of blackmail involves threatening to destroy someone's reputation. Many people are deeply attached to their reputation, making them vulnerable to such blackmail. When they succumb, the blackmailer successfully conquers their target.

Another example is interrogation accompanied by imprisonment or even torture, which was a widespread practice in the Roman Empire. The effectiveness of these methods depends on a person's attachment to their body and their tolerance for pain. Stoics argue that we always have a choice, even in the most horrendous situations. If we yield to the torturer's actions, we consciously choose to be conquered. However, if we refuse to give in despite the excruciating pain, the torturer may harm our bodies but ultimately fails to defeat us.

In *Discourses*, Epictetus repeatedly emphasizes that our ability to choose (or "moral choice," as some scholars translate it, which is part of the ruling-faculty) can never be taken away. In every situation, no matter how dreadful, we have the choice to retain power over our actions or to surrender to circumstances. Epictetus illustrates this power by describing how he would react if a tyrant threatened him:

> *If he says, "I will put you in chains," I reply, "He is threatening my hands and my feet." If he says, "I will behead you," I answer, "He is threatening my neck." If he says, "I will throw you into prison," I say, "He is threatening my whole paltry body;" and if he threatens me with exile, I give the same answer.*

Epictetus, *Discourses*, 1.29 (translated by W.A. Oldfather)

Sounds cool, doesn't it? Epictetus illustrates in this passage that even though the tyrant tries to exercise power over him, he remains unconquerable. Sure, the tyrant can chain his legs, chop his hands, or throw him into prison. But these are simply outside factors that aren't up to him, and thus, according to Epictetus, they're nothing to him. What counts are his actions, and no one but ourselves can decide these.

Enduring hardships

To be unconquerable, there is one condition: we must be willing to endure any hardship. We need to be prepared to completely disregard the opinions of others, to lose everything we possess (even our necessities), to have our bodies confined and mistreated, and to part with everyone we care for. Any strong attachment we hold, anything we are unwilling or unable to let go of, as well as anything we cannot or will not endure, has the potential to destabilize and influence our choices.

An example of being unconquerable (or, at least, pretty close to) is the psychiatrist and philosopher Viktor Frankl, who survived three years of imprisonment in several Nazi concentration camps. In his book *Man's Search for Meaning*, he describes how Jewish prisoners became collaborators with the prison guards, committing terrible acts against their own people in exchange for food and better treatment. Frankl observed how easily individuals succumbed to harsh circumstances and did anything to survive, including betrayal and mistreatment of their own cell mates. But other people refused to let the circumstances influence their values, as they continued acts of kindness and compassion. So, while the Nazis were able to imprison, torture, starve, and exterminate these people, they could not conquer them.

Seneca maintained that hardships themselves are not the problem, but our surrender to them is. Therefore, a Stoic sage will not be disturbed by hardships, meaning they cannot affect him.

> *What element of evil is there in torture and in the other things which we call hardships? It seems to me that there is this evil—that the mind sags, and bends, and collapses. But none of these things can happen to the sage;*

> *he stands erect under any load. Nothing can subdue him; nothing that must be endured annoys him. For he does not complain that he has been struck by that which can strike any man. He knows his own strength; he knows that he was born to carry burdens.*

Lucius Annaeus Seneca, *Moral Letters to Lucilius*, 71.26 (translated by Richard M. Gummere)

Defending our battle lines

Naturally, such a lofty ideal is difficult and nearly impossible to attain. Becoming more unconquerable in the Stoic sense, like anything great, requires practice. The ancient Stoics acknowledged this but encouraged us and themselves to strive for improvement. Additionally, it's tough to be purely 'reasonable' all the time, as our rational faculties don't always have full control over our emotions. The ancient Stoics recognized that emotional reactions initially arise before we can intervene, so even sages are sometimes taken aback. Consequently, they distinguished passions from emotions. According to the Stoics, we have control over our passions: distress, fear, lust, and delight.

So, ideally, the Stoic sage remains free from passions. But most of us aren't sages and will most likely experience strong passions at least from time to time. The good news is that even when our passions strike us, we can still choose. Even if we lay on the ground weeping because of what has overcome us and thus are to a certain extent 'conquered,' we can still decide what we do next. So, we could say there are different defense lines the enemy can cross. The final one is our ability to choose; if someone crosses that line, he has fully conquered us. So, if we want to become unconquerable, we first have to defend our battle lines.

In this analogy, we can defend the line of passions with reason and restraint. Chapter 3: The Passions provides the groundwork for this. We can also defend the line of choice (or moral choice) with the same tools, but it becomes more challenging when the first battle line is breached. If the enemy conquers our emotional state, they will influence our decision-making. For instance, when experiencing strong desire, we are more likely to base our decisions on it, or when angry, we are more likely to act out. Thus, when the enemy stands on our doorstep, we will need firepower to defend our ability to choose.

What is this firepower? We could say it is our inner strength: the power to make the right decision even when overwhelmed by emotion. We see an example of this in the movie *Lord of the Rings* after Frodo accepts an almost impossible mission: to bring the One Ring to Mordor and throw it into the fires of Mount Doom. The danger of the One Ring is its ability to create a strong attachment between itself and the carrier. As a result, the person wearing the ring becomes obsessed and will do anything to avoid separation. Although Frodo eventually succumbs to his attachment, he manages to carry the ring for thousands of miles, overcoming countless moments of temptation. Most other characters—Boromir, for example—would likely have surrendered to the ring much earlier.

Therefore, according to the Stoics, only one thing is genuinely conquerable: our ability to choose. Everything else is outside our control and subject to the whims of fortune. We can lose everything, from our wealth and freedom of movement to our reputations. But our ability to form opinions, desire, hate, accept, abstain, speak, or remain silent remains ours. As Viktor Frankl stated, "When we are no longer able to change a situation, we are challenged to change ourselves."

What happens when we as a whole buckle in and give way to that which seeks to conquer? That's the subject of our next discussion.

Chapter 12   Degenerates

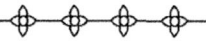

Here is your great soul—the man who has given himself over to Fate; on the other hand, that man is a weakling and a degenerate who struggles and maligns the order of the universe and would rather reform the gods than reform himself.

Lucius Annaeus Seneca, *Moral letters to Lucilius*, 107.12 (translated by Richard M. Gummere)

Imagine a society where everything runs smoothly and harmoniously. People work together, support each other, and enjoy peace and prosperity aside from some minor altercations. But over the years, the values at the core of this society's success begin to fade. People become increasingly unhappy, violent, and hostile towards one another, while love and compassion disappear. This society is now in decline; it's going through a phase of degeneracy.

Similarly, individual people can degenerate. The noun 'degenerate' is commonly used to describe someone who has lost certain qualities considered life-giving. Some forms of degeneracy are natural and unavoidable, like aging and death. But other forms are a consequence of choice, such as how we treat our bodies and minds. In the true sense, 'degeneracy' refers to moral decline and the erosion of values like honesty, integrity, and restraint. From this viewpoint, a 'degenerate' moves below the threshold of an optimal moral state, whatever it may be.

The problem with labeling someone or something morally 'degenerate' is that it's often a subjective matter. For example, someone with very rigid morals and values may view most people as degenerates. But for someone who's more liberal and open-minded, degeneracy may appear much scarcer, or manifest in a completely different manner.

As we saw earlier, the ancient Stoics based their morality on reason and created an ethical system of living in agreement with nature, or a universal rational principle. In chapter 2: Virtues, Vices & Indifferents, we saw how the Stoics viewed a life of virtue as the optimal way to live. It followed that someone who lived a life of vice could be considered a degenerate.

Living in agreement with Zeus

The Stoic's main goal of living in agreement with nature has nothing to do with nature religions, living off-grid, or engaging in primitivism. No, to the Stoics nature in the universe is rational: all events happen according to a well-organized scheme, governed by an impersonal higher power, commonly referred to as 'Zeus' (see chapter 1: *Physics, Ethics & Logic*).

If one doesn't live in accordance with nature, this person leads a morally degenerate existence of vice. Just as virtue can be subdivided into wisdom, justice, courage, and moderation, the opposing system of vice can be subdivided into foolishness, injustice, cowardice, and intemperance. Let's see how these four vices operate.

Foolishness - building sandcastles

Is fate something inexorable or something we can control? Attempting to control fate is like building sandcastles on the beach, expecting the sea not to destroy them. Yet, we often wish for things to happen as we want them to happen, and thus we're disappointed when fate provides us with an unwanted outcome. And so we cry when we lose our jobs, we get angry when someone takes what we believe is ours, and we weep when those we love pass away. But through any resistance or disagreement with the way things happen, we oppose what Seneca called the "Universal Will." So, from this viewpoint, we dispute the inevitable by opposing the divine plan governed by Zeus. We challenge the gods, so to speak, and in doing so, we will always lose.

The quote at the beginning of this chapter is from a letter by Seneca to his friend Lucilius. At the end of this letter, he points out that a degenerate tries to "reform the gods, rather than reform himself." Reforming the gods is an impossible task, and we end up disappointed when we try. After all, they're gods! We can only control our attitude towards them, which, according to the Stoics, should be our primary concern.

Nevertheless, many people spend their lives fighting a losing battle, which is foolish, and foolishness is a Stoic vice. Why fight a battle we can never win? Foolishness is opposed to wisdom and Seneca provides us with a "wiser" approach towards fate:

> *It is to this law that our souls must adjust themselves, this they should follow, this they should obey. Whatever happens, assume that it was bound to happen, and do not be willing to rail at Nature. That which you cannot reform, it is best to endure, and to attend uncomplainingly upon the God under whose guidance everything progresses; for it is a bad soldier who grumbles when following his commander.*

Lucius Annaeus Seneca, *Moral letters to Lucilius*, 107.9 (translated by Richard M. Gummere)

Injustice - the man who cheated

One day, in the ancient Greek city of Nicopolis, a scholar visited one of Epictetus' lectures, where he confessed that he had cheated on his wife. Epictetus criticized the man's behavior harshly by explaining the consequences of not being trustworthy. By committing adultery, we're not just throwing away our "self-respect," "piety," and "fidelity," we also ruin social cohesion and threaten the stability of the state. Epictetus then asked the man how he would wish to be treated. As a neighbor? As a friend? What confidence was he to place in him?

> *And who is going to trust you? Are you not willing, therefore, that you too should be cast forth upon some dunghill as a useless vessel, as a piece of dung? For all that will you say, "Nobody cares for me, a scholar!?" No, for you are an evil man, and useless. It is just as if the wasps complained that nobody cares for them, but all run away from them, and, if anyone can, he strikes them and knocks them down. You have such a sting that you involve in trouble and pain whomever you strike. What do you want us to do with you? There is no place where you can be put.*

Epictetus, *Discourses*, 2.4 (translated by W.A. Oldfather)

To the Stoics, 'justice' is a cardinal virtue, with all its components: piety, honesty, equity, and fair dealing. What Epictetus seems to decry are the consequences of not being just. When there's no justice, society crumbles. If citizens cannot trust each other, how can a nation thrive? And if you aren't trustworthy, of what use are you for the whole?

Now, the Stoic way of handling infidelity seems paradoxical. From the receiving end, if someone cheats on you, it's just another thing beyond our control—that's Fate, and the results of someone else's choices are not up to us. But from the cheater's viewpoint, infidelity is a grave error, showing not just a lack of self-restraint but also an act of injustice. In the Roman Empire, where Epictetus lived, people saw marriage as a sacred institution, and violating it was no small matter.

Cowardice - laying in bed all day

Of course, we require rest to function effectively. However, some people take rest to the next level by sleeping excessively and spending copious amounts of time in a state of idleness. Marcus Aurelius disapproved of such laziness, considering it an unnatural state that conflicts with our intended purpose. In the fifth chapter of *Meditations*, he appears to engage in a debate with himself over the difficulty of rising from bed. Initially, he defends his decision to remain in bed, claiming that "it's nicer." But then he questions himself by asking: "Were you born to feel nice?" Pointing to plants, birds, and ants doing their jobs putting the world in order, he asks "Aren't we supposed to do our tasks as human beings too?" On the other hand, we need to sleep *sometime*, right?

> *Agreed. But nature set a limit on that—as it did on eating and drinking. And you're over the limit. You've had more than enough of that. But not of working. There you're still below your quota. You don't love yourself enough. Or you'd love your nature too, and what it demands of you. People who love what they do wear themselves down doing it; they even forget to wash or eat.*

Marcus Aurelius, *Meditations*, 5.1 (translated by Gregory Hays)

Laziness to the Stoics is a form of cowardice, a *vice*. The opposing virtue is *courage*. If we're lazy, we're not acting in agreement with nature; we're not doing what we're supposed to do. Why do we have muscles? Why do we have a brain? Aren't they meant to be used? As seen, the ultimate state the Stoics want to attain is eudaimonia, a byproduct of living in agreement with nature, a state of *flourishing*, and thus high-mindedness, perseverance, endurance, and cheerfulness. Laziness, sloth, and stagnation are hindrances to a thriving culture.

Intemperance - the sickly pale of lust

"How many are pale from constant pleasures!" remarked Seneca in his essay *On the Shortness of Life*.

Seneca held people driven by lust in low regard, placing them below those who are wrathful, vainglorious, and war mongers: "But among the worst, I count also those who have time for nothing but wine and lust; for none have more shameful engrossments." When someone is enslaved by lust, they are swept away by the whims of Fate, always following that pursuit to satiate their desires above all else. This is a position of weakness, because it lets the outside world wield great power over them.

Seneca's point is that being lustful is a waste of time. Aren't there better ways to spend our lives than pursuing the sensation of the palate, the stimulation of one's sexual organs, or stuffing the mind with useless gossip and pointless entertainment? When our sense of fulfillment depends on satiating our senses, we will spend most of our lives engaged in such pursuits. The problem with this dependency is that the things we need are beyond our control, so we hand over the key to our happiness to Fate. And Fate is ruthless: sometimes it gives us exactly what we want, but often it takes it away just as fast.

> *Many, following no fixed aim, shifting and inconstant and dissatisfied, are plunged by their fickleness into plans that are ever new; some have no fixed principle by which to direct their course, but Fate takes them unawares while they loll and yawn.*

Lucius Annaeus Seneca, *On the Shortness of Life*, chapter II (translated by John W. Basore)

So, when lust possesses us, we not only waste our time in pursuing of pleasure but also place our sense of well-being in the hands of external forces. Moreover, the pursuit of pleasure is a bottomless pit: it's never enough, and we eventually need more to be satisfied, making contentment increasingly complex and time-consuming to find. Our faces become "pale," as we are jaded, insatiable, damaged by excessive consumption, tired, and worn out by the ongoing chase for more. Therefore, from a Stoic perspective, being "chained by lust" is a form of degeneracy because it makes us restless, unfree, and perpetually discontent, besides being damaging to ourselves and often to our surroundings. Intemperance is in conflict with the Stoic virtue of moderation, and Seneca concluded: "Everything in excess becomes a fault."

Chapter 13 Feeling Harmed

The Stoic emperor Marcus Aurelius faced countless challenges during his reign, including wars, political intrigues, the infidelity of his wife Faustina, and the burden of ruling the Roman Empire. He relied on teachers such as his Rusticus, Maximus and Severus. They taught him attributes like self-control, the importance of discipline and optimism in adversity, especially illness.

"Choose not to be harmed—and you won't feel harmed. Don't feel harmed—and you haven't been," wrote Marcus Aurelius. While Marcus' guidance may seem simple in theory, it is difficult to apply without further understanding. For instance, we may ask what triggers our sense of harm, and what wisdom is needed to initiate change?

Fortunately, the ancient Stoics do offer this wisdom. In general, the intensity of human suffering largely depends on the caprices of Fate. However, the degree to which Fate can influence us will vary. A person with a resilient mind would experience less suffering than someone whose emotional wellbeing is wholly reliant on external factors. Certain situations may harm one person while leaving another unaffected. Likewise, many individuals tend to carry the burdens of the past for extended periods, while others manage to shrug them off without allowing the past to sabotage the present and future. Equally common are those who constantly feel threatened by events that have yet to occur—a notion that may seem absurd, but accurately describes chronic worriers.

Ultimately, it isn't the external world or the events within it, including our physical bodies, that cause harm—instead, our thoughts, memories, and fantasies related to them are to blame. Therefore, the secret to resilience lies within our ruling faculties, the sole domain of human experience over which we have total control. This is the value of Stoic philosophy because it concentrates on fortifying the mind, making everything outside it secondary. In this way it can minimize the impact of harmful things on our well-being.

But what tools does Stoicism offer for this endeavor? Marcus Aurelius' writings give us keys. They enable us to view our lives through a different lens and reframe our thoughts about the adversities we encounter, encouraging resilience or, as he phrased it, enabling us to become "like the rock that the waves keep crashing over."

The pain of judgment

Marcus Aurelius declared the mind as sovereign over the soul, a statement that aligns well with Buddhist thought. As the historical Buddha professed, "Nothing precedes the mind." Hence, ultimately, our thoughts determine our feelings. For instance, if we undergo physical pain, we can amplify it by resisting and battling it. We may also create fear atop the pain, obsessing over the prospect that our suffering will never cease or may even intensify in the future. In the end, our thought patterns may inflict more suffering than the physical pain itself.

Marcus Aurelius recommended that our minds should remain "unstirred by agitations of the flesh—gentle and violent ones alike." The exact meaning of "agitations of the flesh" is ambiguous, but the context seems to refer to physical pain and the mind's role in experiencing it. The thought of bodily harm, for instance, is a source of dread for most people, and we generally put in considerable effort to avoid such physical discomfort.

And even though Marcus Aurelius wrote about the agitations of the flesh, we can apply his reasoning to other forms of pain as well. For example, when we find ourselves wounded by an insult, it isn't the insult itself causing the pain, but rather our interpretation of it. Our judgments are dictated by our beliefs. If we hold the belief that no one has the right to insult us, then we'll feel the sting of distress when it happens. However, if we believe that receiving insults is all part of human interaction, and that we lack control over others' actions and words, we're likely to be less disturbed by them.

Regrettably, life offers no assurances that we will forever remain immune to them. It's entirely feasible that we may encounter painful illnesses, accidents, and even fall victim to violence at some point in our lives, so, for the most part, this isn't within our control. Yet, according to Marcus Aurelius, "Nothing happens to anyone that he can't endure." So, although pain is an inescapable aspect of human existence, we can choose whether or not to endure additional pain beyond what the external world imposes on us. The degree of this additional suffering hinges on our judgments.

> *When they make their way into your thoughts, through the sympathetic link between mind and body, don't try to resist the sensation. The sensation is natural. But don't let the mind start in with judgments, calling it "good" or "bad."*

Marcus Aurelius, *Meditations*, 5.26 (translated by Gregory Hays)

Marcus Aurelius draws a clear distinction between sensations and true suffering. Sensations are a natural part of existence; it is the mind that gives birth to suffering. He tells himself not to resist the raw sensation of pain and avoid attaching judgments to it. We might argue that the sensation of pain itself does not automatically equate to suffering, if we don't consider it as something terrible, and accept it as a natural event that is neither good nor bad. "Pain is inevitable; suffering is optional," as the aphorism goes. Alternatively, we could argue that pain in its raw form is quite enough, so why amplify it by resisting it through judgment?

> *Let the part of you that makes that judgment keep quiet even if the body it's attached to is stabbed or burnt, or stinking with pus, or consumed by cancer. Or to put it another way: It needs to realize that what happens to everyone—bad and good alike—is neither good nor bad. That what happens in every life—lived naturally or not—is neither natural nor unnatural.*

Marcus Aurelius, *Meditations*, 4.39 (translated by Gregory Hays)

In short, the root of harm doesn't lie within anyone else's mind, nor does it stem from the fluctuations of the world. It is found in our "capacity to see it."

Are we asking the impossible?

Some people live in continual conflict with the world around them. They are seemingly affected by almost every external event they encounter, be it the news, their neighbors' affairs, or issues at work. Such people can't stop complaining about what's wrong with the world and, in extreme cases, they have convinced themselves that they're better off dead than living in such a miserable place called Earth.

If we live in continual conflict with the world, our beliefs are probably at odds with reality. In many cases, they oppose them. So, if we want to end this ongoing conflict with our environment, we have to change our beliefs. An excellent way to start is to stop expecting so much of the world. In fact, in *Meditations*, Marcus Aurelius argues against asking the impossible, calling it a crazy thing to do. We cannot expect what cannot be delivered, for it's a strategy doomed to fail.

Yet, often in subtle ways, we seem to ask the impossible all the time, as we wish for things to happen that are unrealistic and not in keeping with the nature of the world. So-called 'empty optimists' are prone to this. Their optimism makes them hopeful and confident about a future when there's hardly any ground for it. Confidence and hope aren't bad things in themselves. But if they're not in line with reality, then expect to be disappointed. Expecting nothing but good fortune is asking the impossible. Wishing never to become sick, never be insulted, never be ridiculed is asking the impossible. We have as much control over these things as controlling the tide. For the mind that expects too much, life is continually at fault, as reality never satisfies.

Therefore Marcus Aurelius repeatedly points us to providence. From a Stoic point of view, providence means that nothing happens what nature has not intended.

So, everything we perceive as defects is *intentional* and, therefore, exactly how it should be. Dishonest, arrogant, ungrateful, jealous, and shameless people are part of this world, just like vice, virtue, happiness, sadness, good, and evil. Wishing otherwise would be wishing against nature itself.

> *When you run up against someone else's shamelessness, ask yourself this: Is a world without shamelessness possible? No. Then don't ask the impossible. There have to be shameless people in the world. This is one of them. The same for someone vicious or untrustworthy, or with any other defect.*

Marcus Aurelius, *Meditations*, 9.42 (translated by Gregory Hays)

So, as long as there's life, there will be illness and death. As long as there are people, there will be those with defects. Not asking the impossible is to stop trying to change the universe. We can't do it no matter how much we try. The universe always wins. If we accept this, we'll see the value in lowering our expectations. And if we stop wanting things to happen as we wish but wish for them to happen as they do happen, is there *anything* left that can harm us?

Seeing beauty in adversity

There is an inherent beauty in decay and imperfection that is frequently overlooked. This can be appreciated in the cracks of an aging wall, or the distinctive shapes of older trees; such aspects often pique our interest. Marcus Aurelius mused about loaves of bread that crack open on top in the oven, and how these rough edges, a mere byproduct of baking, stir up a certain appeal and whet the appetite. He stressed the alluring aspect of nature's uncontrolled state. From an aged face to a shriveled apple, or even the ruins of a once-bustling city, we often find such expressions of decay beautiful in their own unique way.

> *And so, if a man has a feeling for, and a deeper insight into the processes of the Universe, there is hardly one but will somehow appear to present itself pleasantly to him, even among mere attendant circumstances. Such a man also will feel no less pleasure in looking at the actual jaws of wild beasts than at the imitations which painters and sculptors exhibit, and he will be enabled to see in an old woman or an old man a kind of freshness and bloom (...).*

Marcus Aurelius, *Meditations*, 3.2 (translated by A.S.L. Farquharson)

So, why don't we treat life's adversities the same way? Life, overall, has a rough side to it. Many things happen that don't comply with our expectations. For example, a fiery romance between two people may promise a beautiful future together but may end up in tears. Or a promising career, backed by all the right qualifications, may come to an end because of illness. And even when our life is a breeze, and everything plays out as had hoped for, we could eventually end up sick and dead. So, we could spend our lives resisting the ugly and be miserable when we experience it, but it's still part of the game.

On the other hand, it's often adversity (not prosperity) that rouses creative people like writers, filmmakers, painters, musicians, and poets, to bring about creations that attract attention. Do you know that Van Gogh only sold one painting, "Red Vineyard at Arles," during his lifetime? Yet, in spite of rejection by the love of his life and people in general, he produced over 900 outstanding works driven by his passion to capture the beauty of landscapes.

Therefore, instead of detesting adversity, we could develop an appreciation for it, like we accept the ridges as part of the bread. The aberrant, the deviant, always accompanies the beautiful. And if we only want the latter and detest the former, we deny Nature as a whole. But if we learn to welcome misfortune as much as a stroke of luck, we'll be less shaken when life gives us lemons.

Misfortune always has a role: it can inspire us, remind us of our fragility, change our perspective on life, and lead us to become more compassionate to others. If we see beauty in whatever overcomes us, Fate will hardly ever harm us.

Focusing on ourselves

As we know that outside circumstances are beyond our control, why do we empower things that we don't have power over by judging them? As a consequence, something that's not up to us can determine how we feel. So, when something that we consider unfavorable enters our lives, we feel bad. And when something that we find desirable leaves us, we feel just as bad. The stronger our judgments are, the more vulnerable we become to the whims of the deity Fortuna, the unpredictable Goddess of luck, chance, and fate.

But Fortuna cannot harm us unless we let her. Not letting Fortuna damage us doesn't mean that we can, somehow, control Fate. Fate will do whatever it wants, and there's nothing we can do about it. But the Stoics emphasized that we do control how we position ourselves towards it. We can resist it, or we can embrace it. This means we can accept what Fortuna provides us with, no matter how unfortunate, and even see beauty in it. Or we can choose to be angry and bitter about it.

There isn't much we can do about the actions of those around us. But it's entirely in our power to focus on ourselves and practice becoming more resilient to the world instead of getting into conflict with it or trying to control it. According to Marcus Aurelius, it's not our problem when, for example, people hate or despise us; "It's their problem." *Our* task is to stay equanimous when facing these people and not being swept away by their malice. And so, we can look at any mishap that's thrown our way. From a Stoic perspective, adversity in itself isn't harmful to our sense of well-being. It's only harmful if we let it be. Hence, Marcus Aurelius wrote: "Choose not to be harmed—and you won't feel harmed. Don't feel harmed—and you haven't been."

One of the aspects of being harmed is the notion of aging. Is there such a thing as aging gracefully?

Chapter 14 Aging

One day, after an extended period away, Seneca returned to his home in the country only to be confronted by its decay. His estate seemed to be falling into ruins, and the once lush garden trees now stood bereft of leaves. His anger was directed towards the landlord who, in response, explained that despite his every effort to preserve the property, the house and trees were simply succumbing to age. Bewildered at how fast his property had fallen apart, the reality of aging became apparent to Seneca.

"Wherever I turn, I see evidence of my advancing years," he wrote to his friend Lucilius. The crumbling stones and the dying trees were proof of how all things decay and that he, himself, was no exception. But instead of being depressed, Seneca decided to cherish old age, stating that it's full of pleasure if one knows how to use it. Two millennia after Seneca walked the earth, people are living longer lifespans, and many often worry about how to spend old age and how to cope with their ebbing vitality. Is life worth living when you're old? According to Seneca, it is.

Why aging isn't so bad

How can anyone possibly enjoy getting older? After all, our bodies are disintegrating, our memory is getting worse by the day, and we cannot function the way we used to. Like children, we're becoming increasingly dependent on other people, sometimes to the point we cannot wash ourselves anymore. How dreadful it is to fall apart, witnessing ourselves getting dragged away from the arena of activity towards the dark pit of eternal non-existence! It's almost as if Fate has given us the best first and saved the worst for last as if being young is to experience and being old to endure.

In his work *On the Shortness of Life*, Seneca wrote how he sees people clinging on to life, wasting their time as if they were still young. He described an older man dying in the act of finally receiving his part of a long-delayed inheritance, and another elder dying amid his duties. It's as if these people spent their days chasing trivialities like wealth and respect, sacrificing their limited time and inner tranquility to obtain these things. Seneca argued that old age has its enjoyments to offer, although they differ from when we were young.

> *Each pleasure reserves to the end the greatest delights which it contains. Life is most delightful when it is on the downward slope, but has not yet reached the abrupt decline. And I myself believe that the period which stands, so to speak, on the edge of the roof, possesses pleasures of its own. Or else the very fact of our not wanting pleasures*

has taken the place of the pleasures themselves. How comforting it is to have tired out one's appetites, and to have done with them!

Lucius Annaeus Seneca, *Moral Letters to Lucilius*, 12.5 (translated by Richard M. Gummere)

When we're young, we tend to chase after pleasures and achievements. Our vitality inclines us to establish ourselves in the world, procreate, and leave a mark. But such desires also have their downsides: they make us restless, and acting upon them will cost us time and energy. In his work *On the Shortness of Life*, Seneca therefore argues that by chasing external things like fame and wealth, people forget to live, and when their time has come, they realize they've spent their time chasing trivialities. During old age, many of these desires erode.

As Seneca mentioned, we're standing *"on the edge of the roof."* If we're standing on the edge, knowing that we could fall anytime, we're probably less interested in adding more money to our fortune or making sure all sorts of people we don't even know pat us on the back. Most important in this situation is the ability to enjoy the time we have left. And so, argues Seneca, merely ceasing the desire for countless pleasures is pleasurable in itself.

Let us cease to desire that which we have been desiring. I, at least, am doing this: in

> *my old age I have ceased to desire what I desired when a boy. To this single end my days and my nights are passed; this is my task, this the object of my thoughts—to put an end to my chronic ills.*
>
> Lucius Annaeus Seneca, *Moral Letters to Lucilius*, 61.1 (translated by Richard M. Gummere)

Celebrating old age

When entering old age, looking back at our younger years tends to evoke feelings of nostalgia. Life used to be beautiful and vibrant when we still had energetic, strong bodies. The world was our oyster; a whole life was spread in front of us, with countless possibilities. But now, our lives have passed to a great extent. We've made our choices, and had our chances. Some things turned out to be as we expected; other things failed. But most of us have accumulated a collection of life experiences (good and bad) when we reach old age. According to Seneca, the fact that we have lived is a reason for celebration *on its own*. We've had happy, enjoyable moments to reflect on and for which we can be grateful. We may also have had periods of hardship, and we can be satisfied and proud we've managed to endure them.

In one of his letters, Seneca recounted the peculiar custom of Pacuvius, the legate and governor who acquired ownership of the province of Syria. Pacuvius had a habit of regularly staging his own funeral feast, a spectacle complete with traditional mourning rites. As his servants carried him from the dining room to his quarters amidst music and applause, they would chant: "He has lived his life, he has lived his life!" Drawing inspiration from the governor's ritual, Seneca proposed that we should regularly remind ourselves of the life course we have already traversed, as set out for us by fortune.

> *That man is happiest, and is secure in his own possession of himself, who can await the morrow without apprehension. When a man has said: 'I have lived!' every morning he arises he receives a bonus.*

Lucius Annaeus Seneca, *Moral Letters to Lucilius*, 12.9 (translated by Richard M. Gummere)

Seneca advised that we should approach each day as if it were our last—"as if it rounded out and completed our existence." Perceiving our lives as products of Fate, we come to understand that we haven't been short-changed, and that all has transpired according to a greater plan. Standing on the precipice, we patiently await the moment we plunge into the void, cherishing every additional second bestowed upon us by Fate as a victory. And when we finally descend, we can confidently declare "I have lived" and face the abrupt ending with satisfaction.

I am endeavouring to live every day as if it were a complete life. I do not indeed snatch it up as if it were my last; I do regard it, however, as if it might even be my last.

Lucius Annaeus Seneca, *Moral Letters to Lucilius*, 61.1 (translated by Richard M. Gummere)

Falling off the edge

The inevitable destination of old age is death. However, the idea of plummeting into oblivion fills many of us with fear and apprehension. As we all know, the eventual fall is inevitable; we just don't know precisely when it happens. As we advance in years, time confronts us with the approaching end. Our vitality wanes, our bodies deteriorate, all while newer, more vigorous generations take the reins. And so, we try to extend our youth, which may work for a while. But, eventually, the degeneracy of age begins to burst at the seams. The prospect of falling off the edge becomes more robust, more visible, and daunting to many.

It's one thing to celebrate having lived; it's another to embrace the fact that the life we celebrate is ending. Yet, resisting this reality amounts to defying Fate. We can't escape death, as it's part of life. In a letter to Lucilius, Seneca proclaimed he was ready to depart. "Dying well means dying gladly," he stated. This doesn't mean that he actively pursued death but that he cheerfully accepted his mortality. His readiness, so he argued, relieved him of his anxiety, making his life's last chapters even more enjoyable. Seneca urged never to do anything unwillingly. If we welcome whatever Fate brings, we will never act against our will, because our desire will be not for things to transpire as we wish, but as they indeed happen—and this includes death.

> *The man who does something under orders is not unhappy; he is unhappy who does something against his will. Let us therefore so set our minds in order that we may desire whatever is demanded of us by circumstances, and above all that we may reflect upon our end without sadness.*

Lucius Annaeus Seneca, *Moral Letters to Lucilius*, 61.3 (translated by Richard M. Gummere)

Being ready

Is Seneca telling us to give up on life then? No, he didn't write that. He *did* write that we should be ready for death and embrace its coming. We should not abandon the act of living but be relieved of anxiety by accepting and embracing our limited time on Earth. How can we celebrate that we've lived if we're crippled by fear of the inevitable end? Moreover, the less time we've got left and the closer we come to death, the more *reason we have* to seize the day, as the chances of it *being* our last increase steadily.

In addition, Seneca seems to advocate a realistic attitude towards old age. There are many things we can't do anymore and many we don't even desire to do. We can accept our limitations and adapt ourselves to life's circumstances, or we can make life a miserable experience by spending our last days beating our heads against a stone wall. Old age grants us many opportunities, like the enjoyment of pleasant memories. We can find serenity in no longer having to go through many adversities and tribulations that come with life anymore; we've done that and survived. In fact, having resigned from many things and having ceased desiring many others leaves the elderly an excellent opportunity to study philosophy.

Chapter 15 Self-Discipline

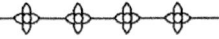

The modern landscape of the internet inundates us with motivational quotes and videos designed to spur us into action. However, motivation is only the spark that gets us started; to truly achieve something, we must commit to the work. The journey towards any significant goal, such as mastering driving or completing an academic education, calls for effort and perseverance. Despite a few exceptions, there rarely exist shortcuts to such accomplishments. We could be brimming with motivation, but without action, we won't get anywhere.

Many people struggle with engaging in repetitive cycles over a period necessary to achieve their goals. They have the intention, the desire, but no meaningful forward momentum. These individuals lack what is likely the missing key to unlocking achievement: self-discipline. Self-discipline is a controlled effort that requires self-restraint and obedience to specific rules—like a schedule. Discipline generally gets a bad rap, as it sounds unromantic and tiresome and reminds us of the strict regimes of militaries and boarding schools. But it gets the job done. Furthermore, self-discipline often fosters inner peace, as its inherent structure and predictability alleviate the stress generated by uncertainty.

The Stoics considered discipline a virtue, along with other related qualities like perseverance, endurance, high-mindedness, and self-control. The Stoics favored hard work and spending their days wisely. Seneca, for example, urges us not to waste our time and to act now as life is short. Marcus Aurelius turns to nature as his guide, concluding that we are naturally inclined towards industriousness.

The Cambridge dictionary describes self-discipline as "the ability to make yourself do things you know you should do even when you do not want to." Making oneself do certain things requires self-control to resist engaging in activities that don't contribute to our goals. Also, it requires drive to perform our daily tasks and a target to work towards. So, if we do what we should do and refrain from what we shouldn't, we're disciplined. This sounds easy, but for many, it isn't.

Three dimensions: *self-control*, *work,* and *aim* were praised by the ancient Stoics for contributing to self-discipline. Even though the Stoics sought inner peace, they weren't lazy: they knew that living in agreement with nature meant, for us, humans, using our bodies and minds appropriately by being productive, active, and contributing to the whole. We're not to waste our inherent attributes; we ought to use them properly.

Epictetus argued that the engagement in adversities was what made Hercules Hercules. What would have become of him if he had not used his powerful physique and noble soul? The world offered him challenges that called a strong man like Hercules to take up, as he was built for them and not for snoring away his life. By following his natural inclinations, he not only developed into a hero, he also contributed to society by getting rid of many dangers to his people. It was a win-win situation.

The power of self-control

Self-control is therefore a vital part of being self-disciplined. Through self-control, we can restrain ourselves from not doing things we shouldn't be doing. Working towards a specific goal, for example, or writing a thesis is theoretically a simple task. We just need to put in the necessary hours of research and writing to finish it. However, in reality, people struggle with such an undertaking. For a significant part, this struggle exists because of how they handle distractions.

Unfortunately, we have no control over the distractions that swarm around us. As Epictetus mentions, things not in our control do not constitute our own actions. But we do have control over how we position ourselves towards the things we cannot control. In the case of distractions, we can't control invites for drinks, the release of the latest season of our favorite television series, or people trying to bring us down by criticizing and opposing us. No matter how much we try to resist, the world will always have plenty of things to offer that potentially grab our attention and persuade us to change our minds about our choices. It's probably only increasing due to technological developments. Of course, we can influence the number of distractions we're exposed to by limiting our contact with the outside world and rearranging our living environment. But, ultimately, the outside world, including our immediate environment, is up to Fate.

So, what can we do? Strengthen our self-control. We can bolster ourselves against inevitable distractions, reinforcing our resolve to finish what we wish to finish. If we have the strength to reject what's set before us, temptations will not sway us from our cause.

But self-control takes practice; we must master it through exposure and repetition, so we fortify our ability to restrain. The more we conquer distractions and temptations, the less powerful they become. If these temptations have no (or limited) power over us, we can experience what the Stoics call freedom. Within the context of discipline, it's the freedom to do what we *intend* to do so that outside circumstances do not control our actions.

Industriousness: a Stoic virtue

How can we get things done if we're not able or willing to work for it? From the Stoic perspective of human nature, work is not only important, it's also what we're designed to do. The ancient Stoics believed that everything in the universe has its place, and as humans, we're granted unique capabilities to serve the whole. Therefore, industriousness a virtuous characteristic: it's in our DNA to work.

In *Meditations*, Marcus Aurelius repeatedly reminds himself of his tasks as emperor and as a human being. He's here to work and to serve, not to lay in bed all day doing nothing.

> *At dawn, when you have trouble getting out of bed, tell yourself: "I have to go to work—as a human being. What do I have to complain of, if I'm going to do what I was born for—the things I was brought into the world to do? Or is this what I was created for? To huddle under the blankets and stay warm?"*

Marcus Aurelius, *Meditations*, 5.1 (translated by Gregory Hays)

Yes, it may feel much nicer to stay in bed in winter. But the Stoic emperor reminds himself that he was not born to feel "nice." He mentions how plants, sparrows, ants, spiders, and bees perform their tasks, working to put their world in order in ways that nature has assigned to them. "Why aren't you running to do what your nature demands?" he asks himself. Of course, we can't work all day. "Nature set a limit on that—as it did on eating and drinking," He states. So, there's a time for relaxation and a time for work.

As mentioned before, 'courage' is a cardinal virtue in Stoicism that can be subdivided into endurance, confidence, high-mindedness, cheerfulness, and industriousness. *Industriousness* is a vital part of being self-disciplined. It's the habit of being active and occupied. If we're working towards a goal, self-control alone isn't enough; we need to be industrious and do what needs to be done consistently. But how can we be industrious? How can we prevent ourselves from being lazy and procrastinating?

Marcus Aurelius makes a hard-hitting statement about the cause of laziness:

> *You don't love yourself enough. Or you'd love your nature too, and what it demands of you. People who love what they do wear themselves down doing it, they even forget to wash or eat. Do you have less respect for your own nature than the engraver does for engraving, the dancer for the dance, the miser for money or the social climber for status?*

Marcus Aurelius, *Meditations*, 5.1 (translated by Gregory Hays)

According to this passage, laziness means a lack of love for oneself or one's natural tendencies. A lazy person doesn't love that he's naturally inclined to be industrious; if he did, he'd embrace his nature and get to work. So, extrapolating from this idea, we might want to stimulate our love of being industrious; instead of seeing it as a form of punishment or condemnation, we might want to see it as something enjoyable. After all, it has been a natural, inherent part of human life since the dawn of time, in different forms and intensities. We also might want to seek something that complements our individual natures. It was befitting of Hercules, for example, to protect the weak because of his strong, athletic body. Other people might be better fit for writing, art, or scientific pursuits. Nature has given each of us unique characteristics, which from a Stoic point of view, we should honor and use productively to serve the whole.

The star in the sky

As Seneca made clear, life is short, and we're wasting most of it. How many people wander through life without any aim, without any overarching goal to point their energy towards? To truly get going, we need a finish line to run towards; we need that star in the sky, whatever it may be, to climb towards. The easiest way to live an undisciplined life is not having a specific goal. If we don't have goals or sub-goals, we're quick to put our energy into things that don't serve anything long-term—or we do not act at all. As Marcus Aurelius stated:

> *But make sure you guard against the other kind of confusion. People who labor all their lives but have no purpose to direct every thought and impulse toward are wasting their time—even when hard at work.*

Marcus Aurelius, *Meditations*, 2.7 (translated by Gregory Hays)

In the modern world, we may wear ourselves out by partying, drinking, playing video games excessively, or binge-watching television. It's not that we're not doing anything; we just spend our time and energy on, mainly, short-term pleasures, and we work simply to keep riding the hamster wheel of small pleasures and consumer appetites. To many people, life seems pointless, and striving for something bigger, like realizing their dreams and ambitions, seems impossible. But, most likely, they're missing *aim*, which could be because of fear of failure, but also because nowadays, there are so many options that it's difficult to choose *one* direction to go. The paradox of choice confuses many and causes people to want countless things, but end up with nothing substantial. Therefore, choosing one particular goal and letting everything else slide benefits those drifting in the wastelands of modernity.

Marcus Aurelius stated:

> *Stop drifting—sprint to the finish. Write off your hopes, and if your well-being matters to you, be your own savior while you can.*

Marcus Aurelius, *Meditations*, 3.14 (translated by Gregory Hays)

Will we, out of our own aimlessness, let others make choices for us, even though we can make our own? Will we travel aimlessly—or rather "be traveled" — through life like leaves in the wind? Or will we exploit our *only true power*, which is our ability to choose and act?

To conclude, self-discipline becomes much easier if we have a strong and clear aim. We generate purpose for ourselves by embracing a solid reason for getting out of bed every morning. And the more we work towards that goal, the more steadfast we generally become. As we keep an eye on the finish line, seeing it getting closer every day, we build self-confidence as we realize that we *can* get things done. Observing our progress motivates us to continue. It prevents us from drifting aimlessly from one hunch to another. We'll get things done, even if we don't want to, because that star in the sky shines brightly above us and rises far above everything that doesn't matter, leaving that in the shade where it belongs.

Chapter 16 Future, Past, Present

Marcus Aurelius, once the most powerful man in the known world, attempted to live virtuously following Stoic principles. Unlike many Roman Emperors, he did not indulge in the many pleasures he had access to, like getting drunk on wine and watching sadistic games in the Colosseum. He purposed to fulfill the task Fortuna had given him: serving humanity. So, he cared deeply about fulfilling his purpose. But to do so, he had to care less about the things that are neither worthy nor wise to care about. And these are many.

As we've seen, one of the essential concepts in Stoicism is the schism between things we control and do not control. Most (if not all) things beyond our own actions are not up to us. Does that mean we should renounce the world? Not necessarily. But the Stoics believed that we should be realistic about our limited influence on these things and that we create an unnecessary burden for ourselves if we are not.

When life hurts, it often means that we care about things we have no control over, and by doing so, we let them control us and play with us like puppeteers. Then, we blame the puppeteers for pulling our strings while, in actuality, we give them leave to do so. But if we stop caring about them so much, they lose power over us, and we'll be undisturbed. For Marcus Aurelius, being unperturbed by things outside of his control allowed him to cope with the many responsibilities and challenges he faced as an emperor and to focus on the task he believed he was given by the gods. For Epictetus, it meant freedom. For other people, it could be not being moved by external forces (or a selection of them) and focusing on goals that *do* matter. And for others, it could simply be a path to a happy, carefree life.

When life hurts, what are the things we should stop occupying ourselves with? And how do we do it? In *Meditations*, Marcus Aurelius repeatedly differentiates between *present*, *past*, and *future*. In each category, the ancient Roman Emperor has valuable things to say about how we care too much about them, or in the wrong ways, or about the wrong things.

(1) The future

As Seneca has shown us, we suffer more in our imagination than in reality, implying that our thoughts are the source of our suffering. When it comes to the future, our imagination often goes wild, inventing countless scenarios of what could happen (but probably never will). Beforehand, we think of ways to handle possible outcomes while shivering because of the thought of "not knowing how the future will eventually play out." In some instances, what happens is indeed what we anticipate. But in many other instances, Fate surprises us, overwhelming us with events we couldn't have anticipated.

Marcus Aurelius wrote that it's not the future pressing down on us but only the present. It's not the future that hurts us but how we deal with it in the *present*. The misery of the future happens *in the present*. And, ironically, it's not the future unfolding in the present. No, the misery of the future is our worrying about it *now*. When we care too much about future events, life eventually begins to hurt as we suffer them in our imagination, and let them dictate our present.

Antidote

So, what does Marcus Aurelius say about being too concerned about the future? First, let's consider the following passage:

> *Let not the future trouble you; for you will come to it, if come you must, bearing with you the same reason which you are using now to meet the present.*

Marcus Aurelius, *Meditations*, 7.8 (translated by A.S.L. Farquharson)

He pointed out that if he could cope with the present, he could also cope with the future. He told himself not to picture everything dreadful that could happen but instead stick with the situation at hand. When he focused on the present, he realized he could bear it. And if that's the case, why wouldn't he be able to handle what's yet to come? This attitude resembles the idea of *Amor Fati*, the love of Fate, but we are then fortified with the trust that we'll be able to get through it.

(2) The past

Marcus Aurelius again reminded himself of how fast existence passes by and disappears into the infinite before we can grasp it. Like the future, the past is a realm we cannot operate in. What's gone is gone, and unless we invent the time machine, we can't change anything about it. He stated:

> *Forget everything else. Keep hold of this alone and remember it: Each of us lives only now, this brief instant. The rest has been lived already, or is impossible to see. The span we live is small—small as the corner of the earth in which we live it.*

Marcus Aurelius, *Meditations*, 3.10 (translated by Gregory Hays)

So, to be comfortable we need to acknowledge the 'narrowness' of our lives, and stay within the confines of the present moment. However, we're often overly occupied with those areas that lie outside of it and cannot be entered: the future and the past. Marcus Aurelius stated that the past "signifies as much as nothing and is at present indifferent." It's not that events in the past don't influence the present or that we cannot learn from past events. It's just that we cannot work with the past—it's already out of our reach. And often, our memories of the past are scrambled, and ways of verifying what exactly happened are limited. We rely on recollections from personal perspectives and different viewpoints of ourselves or others. So, the past is not only out of reach; our remembrance of it is most likely inaccurate.

Yet, we keep caring about past events, often repeating them in our minds, rehearsing the pain they caused us. Some believe that by thinking about the past, we may have some control over it. But that's an illusion. The past is gone. All we can try to control are our thoughts about something that's been flushed away, never to return. "I wish I could have done this differently," many people say. But they are wishing for the impossible. Nothing can be gained from such thoughts, as they evoke desires we can never fulfill.

Antidote

Instead of focusing on the past events in themselves, Marcus Aurelius focused on his reaction toward them. Granted we cannot control past events—*we* couldn't even prevent them when they occurred in the present—but we can control how we position ourselves toward these events. Initially, we might consider the past unfortunate. We might have had difficult childhoods or experienced the ending of friendships or failed business ventures. But, according to Marcus Aurelius, the nature of these events isn't so important; what counts is what we have learned from them and how they have contributed to our growth. He stated:

> *It's unfortunate that this has happened. No. It's fortunate that this has happened and I've remained unharmed by it—not shattered by the present or frightened of the future. It could have happened to anyone. But not everyone could have remained unharmed by it. Why treat the one as a misfortune rather than the other as fortunate? Can you really call something a misfortune that doesn't violate human nature? Or do you think something that's not against nature's will can violate it? But you know what its will is. Does what's happened keep you from acting with justice, generosity, self-control, sanity, prudence, honesty, humility, straightforwardness, and all the other qualities that allow a person's nature to fulfill itself?*

Marcus Aurelius, *Meditations*, 4.49a (translated by Gregory Hays)

So, Marcus Aurelius didn't discard the value of the past. He believed we could learn from the past by looking at its rhythm: how things come and go, repeating themselves, so we can "extrapolate" the future.

(3) The present

Marcus Aurelius frequently mentions that the present moment is all we have: it's the narrow field we have access to. From the present, we can stare into the endless abyss of the past and the impenetrable darkness of the future. From this perspective, he encouraged himself to stick with what was in his control: *this moment*.

But even when we let go of the past and minimize our worries about the future, we may still very well care too much about things not worthy of concern: the things happening *as we speak*. We are often dissatisfied with the ways life is playing out in the moment. And when things don't go as we wish, we tend to get angry, sad, or depressed. But according to Marcus Aurelius, being emotionally disturbed by what external circumstances throw at us is pointless.

How the world around us unfolds itself is not up to us—how we react to it is. Yet, we tend to get disturbed because we don't like what's happening or what we want to happen doesn't happen. Marcus Aurelius stated that we shouldn't fight what we're compelled to. He compared people who struggle with Fate to pigs, kicking and squealing when sacrificed: it's no use, as we can't avoid what the gods have in store. We cannot stop people from wanting to fight wars; we cannot stop natural disasters from happening; we cannot prevent our bodies from aging. In the same way, we cannot force the world to grant us our wishes; we're not guaranteed that the people we're attracted to are also attracted to us, nor assured that all human beings have the same shots at life. All that is just not possible.

Antidote

Marcus Aurelius saw the law of nature as our master. If we run from it or feel grief or anger about it, we're nothing more than deserters and fugitives. We must accept the ways of nature, embrace them, and focus on dealing with them instead of wasting our energy being disgusted by or clinging to our circumstances. Marcus Aurelius' solution is to accept the present, arguing that we should focus on what we have, not what we lack, but with caution.

> *Treat what you don't have as nonexistent. Look at what you have, the things you value most, and think of how much you'd crave*

> *them if you didn't have them. But be careful.*
> *Don't feel such satisfaction that you start to*
> *overvalue them—that it would upset you to*
> *lose them.*

Marcus Aurelius, *Meditations*, 7.27 (translated by Gregory Hays)

Nevertheless, accepting one's circumstances can be difficult; especially when we face significant hardships repeatedly. Can't we just have a break? But to Marcus Aurelius, adversity is not an excuse to behave like squealing pigs. Rather, it's an opportunity to "practice virtue," in other words, to apply Stoic philosophy to one's life. The art of living isn't about how amazing and fortunate our external circumstances are, as they're unreliable, weak, fickle, and not our own. It's about how we face the events we meet; that's what we should care about. As Marcus Aurelius stated:

> *Because to me the present is a chance for the*
> *exercise of rational virtue—civic virtue—in*
> *short, the art that men share with gods. Both*
> *treat whatever happens as wholly natural;*
> *not novel or hard to deal with, but familiar*
> *and easily handled.*

Marcus Aurelius, *Meditations*, 7.68 (translated by Gregory Hays)

What further insights can we gain from studying the works of this remarkable man? Though he was emperor, he never abused his position and, though he never claimed to be a philosopher, pondered deeply on life.

Chapter 17   Embrace Fate and Live Well

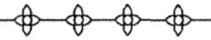

Though he never called himself a philosopher, Marcus Aurelius' writings have evolved into some of the most revered ancient Stoic texts. His *Meditations* comprises a compilation of personal reflections rooted in Stoic concepts, one of which highlights the acceptance of Fate and nature's demands. Rather than yearning for events to happen according to our desires, Marcus Aurelius proposes that we are better served by accepting the universe as it is, cultivating adaptability towards external circumstances while maintaining our virtues.

Yet, most of us want our lives to be pleasant and expect our environment to provide us with what we need to feel content. We want friendly people around us, we want to achieve our dreams and ambitions, remain youthful, and live without misfortune. At the same time, we're often not content with our bodies and inborn talents and refuse to accept our flaws.

In essence, being human involves a considerable amount of 'wanting' (particularly in our present consumerist society), contrasted with minimal 'accepting' of external situations. However, the more we expect from the universe, the more susceptible we are to disappointment. Despite our best efforts, we are likely to encounter disagreeable individuals, fall short of achieving our dreams and aspirations, face adversities, and inevitably fail to evade aging. If these inescapable experiences cause us distress, we become puppets of our surroundings, emotionally hinged on its vagaries.

In *Meditations*, Marcus Aurelius repeatedly encouraged himself to *embrace* Fate precisely the way it comes and live well regardless of the circumstances. This final chapter, based on the memoirs of the Stoic emperor, explores why accepting the universe rather than opposing and trying to change it might be the better option. Here are some practical observations.

(1) Accepting other people

Dealing with other people means dealing with the unpredictable and uncontrollable. Some people are good and moral, others are evil and immoral; some are hardworking and helpful, and others are lazy and exploitative. Some like to make jokes; others are quick to use violence. Marcus Aurelius emphasized that regardless of people being arrogant, ungrateful, deceitful, and unsocial, we all share the same nature of being *human*. Human nature consists of beauty *and* ugliness, so he encouraged himself to accept everyone and not be perturbed by evil people.

In his mind, we're here to cooperate, not act against each other (which is contrary to nature). We may desire people to behave in a certain manner, but the reality is that people possess their own free will, and how they conduct themselves is beyond our control. We can attempt to influence them, yet, in the end, they'll express their thoughts and do what they deem fit, no matter how irrational or absurd it may seem. Consequently, expending precious energy in trying to alter them is a futile endeavor, and is better redirected elsewhere.

> *Don't waste the rest of your time here worrying about other people—unless it affects the common good. It will keep you from doing anything useful. You'll be too preoccupied with what so-and-so is doing, and why, and what they're saying, and what they're thinking, and what they're up to, and all the other things that throw you off and keep you from focusing on your own mind.*

Marcus Aurelius, *Meditations*, 3.4 (translated by Gregory Hays)

(2) Accepting transience

The Stoic emperor was intensely aware of how temporary things are and how quickly things we now regard as significant turn into ghosts of the past. Looking at the great emperors and philosophers of old, important, people of renown that used to walk the earth but have been reduced to dust and ashes. Children can be compared to leaves in the wind, which grow in spring but are then blown away, and the forest then replaces them with new ones. Just as leaves bud and fall, so do generations of humans come and go. We originate from a speck of semen, and before we know it, we draw our last breath.

Everything is ephemeral, and our existence is but a fleeting moment, particularly when juxtaposed with the lifespan of our planet (let alone the universe). As Marcus Aurelius phrased it:

> *Forget everything else. Keep hold of this alone and remember it: Each of us lives only now, this brief instant. The rest has been lived already or is impossible to see. The span we live is small—small as the corner of the earth in which we live it. Small as even the greatest renown, passed from mouth to mouth by short-lived stick figures, ignorant alike of themselves and those long dead.*

Marcus Aurelius, *Meditations*, 3.10 (translated by Gregory Hays)

For some, the reality of transience may be a source of suffering. Isn't it sad that death takes us back so shortly after we come into existence? Hence, some people desperately cling to life and seek ways to extend it beyond its natural span, looking for the fountain of eternal youth. All such attempts to go against nature are in vain, as we're given just a limited amount of time here, the greater part of which is spent in bodily decay.

But there's also a positive side to the transient nature of the universe: it's the thought that because nothing lasts, nothing is worthy of worry. As an example, Marcus Aurelius described the futility of seeking the praises of man:

> *But look at how soon we're all forgotten. The abyss of endless time that swallows it all. The emptiness of all those applauding hands. The people who praise us—how capricious they are, how arbitrary. And the tiny region in which it all takes place. The whole earth a point in space— and most of it uninhabited.*

Marcus Aurelius, *Meditations*, 4.3 (translated by Gregory Hays)

The more we realize how little and short our lives are, the less reason we see to worry about trivialities, and the more we can appreciate the time we have. Moreover, from a Stoic point of view, the shortness of life is also a reason *not to waste time*. Whatever we want to do, now is the moment.

(3) Accepting misfortune

We could wish and pray for misfortune never to occur, but looking at reality, we see that no one escapes the darker sides of existence. Adversity is part of life. If we fight against it, we don't just experience misfortune itself but also the disappointment of encountering it despite our wish not to. In accordance with Stoic cosmology, all events in your life can be attributed to the gods: the origin of all entities. Circumstances may arise that appear tragic, but according to the Stoics, it's in alignment with the gods' intentions. Thus, for instance, the ending of a relationship is part of the divine plan, and no amount of prayer can prevent it.

Hence, Marcus Aurelius would suggest it would be better to direct our prayers to things we *can* control.

> *Start praying like this and you'll see. Not "some way to sleep with her"—but a way to stop wanting to. Not "some way to get rid of him"—but a way to stop trying. Not "some way to save my child"—but a way to lose your fear. Redirect your prayers like that, and watch what happens.*

Marcus Aurelius, *Meditations*, 9.40 (translated by Gregory Hays)

We can't control the actions of a romantic partner, but we can work on ourselves, building mental fortitude for enduring a possible breakup. We can't prevent someone we're attached to from walking out of our lives, but we can develop the power to accept whatever happens and even *wish* for things to happen as they happen. If we accept misfortune, even the gods cannot harm us, no matter what they put on the table.

(4) Accepting change as the order of things

We've explored transience earlier, but 'change' is different. Change isn't just the *temporary nature* of all things, but the *entire process* of things becoming different. There's never a fixed state in the universe, so the process of change is always at work. Even the most unchanging objects like a calm landscape or rock steadily resting in the surf are changing, even though less visibly than, let's say, our lips when talking or someone's posture when running.

Nature inherently embodies change; everything stems from it, and nothing in the world remains static. Not only does the universe around us undergo change, but we too transform, as evidenced by the cells in our bodies that incessantly regenerate until we die. Marcus Aurelius described 'change' as the natural order of things that ultimately benefits the whole. We could compare the changes we see around us to our bodies constantly replacing old parts with new ones; this may be unfortunate for the pieces in themselves, but good for the body altogether. In the same way, our environment engages in enduring self-maintenance, replacing old with new elements, always seeking the optimal balance.

It's all about the unfolding of nature's plan, and we should accept it, according to Marcus Aurelius, as it leads to "the good health of the world, and the well-being and prosperity of Zeus himself."

We saw how some living creatures come into existence and die within twenty-four hours, like the mayfly. Others live for more than 10,000 years, like the glass sponge. Many planets survive billions of years. But none of these things are eternal, for, as change gives birth to them, it will also destroy them. Without change, our world wouldn't exist, and life wouldn't be possible. As Marcus Aurelius concluded, "The world is nothing but change."

But, ironically, even though we're born out of change, we *fear* change at the same time. Many people cling to situations, objects, people, and ideas, wishing they'd never change, always stay the same. But the change they so intensely fear is already in progress, and the moment of witnessing these alterations with our bare eye is just a matter of time. When the sun shines, a storm is on its way; when it's summer, the fall is already knocking on its door. Trying to maintain the status quo is like grasping water, expecting it never to flow out of your hands.

Some things are rushing into existence, others out of it. Some of what now exists is already gone. Change and flux constantly remake the world, just as the incessant progression of time remakes eternity. We find ourselves in a river. Which of the things around us should we value when none of them can offer a firm foothold? Like an attachment to a sparrow: we glimpse it and it's gone.

Marcus Aurelius, *Meditations* 6.15 (translated by Gregory Hays)

(5) Accepting your nature

Many people have difficulty accepting their natural attributes, such as their appearance, physical weaknesses, and even the unavoidable Fate of aging and death. But Marcus Aurelius encouraged himself to accept the limits placed on his body and be content with his days. He also told himself to remember the nature of the world, his nature, how he relates to the world, and that he is part of nature and expected to live in harmony with it.

Some people have more athletic bodies and "Herculean strength" (as Epictetus put it); others have greater intellects. It is possible to stretch ourselves beyond our innate capabilities. But we're also confined to certain natural limitations: first and foremost, the limitation of being human. The Stoics emphasized that one unique feature of human nature is our faculty of reason unlike any other sentient being on Earth, enabling us to transcend our brute nature. So, instead of being servants to our passions, we have the power to override them with reason.

Marcus Aurelius was a man who used reason to accept the world around him, good and bad, despite the persuasions of his more carnal nature and disappointments in life. Here is a person we can all relate to and emulate.

Printed in Great Britain
by Amazon